THE SEPTUAGINT

H. D. Williams, M.D., Ph.D.

THE CHARACTER OF GOD'S WORDS

IS NOT FOUND IN THE SEPTUAGINT THE SO-CALLED LXX

by
H. D. Williams, M.D., Ph.D.

Disclaimer

The author of this work has quoted the writers of many articles and books. This does not mean that the author endorses or recommends the works of others. If the author quotes someone, it does not mean that he agrees with all of the author's tenets, statements, concepts, or words, whether in the work quoted or any other work of the author. There has been no attempt to alter the meaning of the quotes; and therefore, some of the quotes are long in order to give the entire sense of the passage.

Copyright © 2019 by H. D. Williams
All Rights Reserved
Printed in the United States of America

Library of Congress Control Number: 2007942449
REL006201: Religion: Biblical Studies - Topical

ISBN 978-1-7339247-3-3

All Scripture quotes are from the King James Bible except those verses compared and then the source is identified.

No part of this work may be reproduced without the expressed consent of the publisher, except for brief quotes, whether by electronic, photocopying, recording, or information storage and retrieval systems.

Address All Inquiries To:
THE OLD PATHS PUBLICATIONS, Inc.
142 Gold Flume Way
Cleveland, Georgia, U.S.A.

Web: www.theoldpathspublications.com
E-mail: TOP@theoldpathspublications.com

This work was written in 2008 and published as an ebook, but so many have called for a printed book, we have acquiesced to the requests.

DEDICATION

This work is dedicated to my wife, Patricia, who has been by my side through good and bad times. She is far more precious than rubies. She has never been a spendthrift, even during times of plenty, and is always content, no matter the circumstances. (Proverbs 31)

FOREWORD

This little book was written in 2008 and made available by download from our publishing website. Over the years many have requested a copy that could be held in their hands.

So, "The Old Paths Publications, Inc." has decided to publish the work. Since it was first made available, I have discovered that there is another twist to the account of the Septuagint.

Those who have fallen into the trap of a "pre" A.D. LXX, a Greek translation of the Old Testament before the incarnation of the Lord Jesus Christ, are primarily Roman Catholic expositors. Now they are promoting yet another a false claim. Specifically, they claim the chronology in the mystical Septuagint, the LXX, is more accurate than the Traditional Masoretic Text as accurately and faithfully translated into the King James Version. Dr. Phil Stringer reports in a video of a message presented to the King James Bible Research Council a few years ago:

> The recent attacks on the KJB are coming primarily from Roman Catholic websites.

And paraphrasing his comments:

> The method being used is to attack the **chronology** of the events recorded in the Masoretic text. In short, they claim the MT is wrong, but the LXX is right. They claim the modus operandi of "the RC intellectuals" (because if you support the KJB, you are a cultic member or just plain dumb) is correct. The "doctors" of the RC desire to destroy the Hebrew Masoretic text upon which the KJB is translated. Subsequently, they claim the new

5

THE CHARACTER OF GOD'S WORDS IS NOT IN THE "LXX"

> versions are correct, Jesus and the apostles quoted from the LXX, the LXX was before Christ and He used it, so all the reasoning behind the KJB translation is false. All the catholic scholars say this. So, if you disagree you must be wrong.
>
> Listening to the "concept modernist" (those who believe the Words of the Bible are not preserved, there is no verbal inspiration and preservation, rather only the concept has been retained) they are right because of their penchant to follow a false letter, without any evidence to support their stand. In other words, whether they have facts or not, we are wrong.

In response to the Roman Catholic "intellectuals," I quote from one of the best Bible scholars, Dr. J. A. Moorman, who wrote a comprehensive work on Bible Chronology.

> The Bible's chronology as with all else in Scripture is given and preserved by the Holy Spirit. Chronology gives the Bible its form, its structure, its actuality. The Bible can be tested in all points, and so in the subject before us it can be tested as regards time. Our study here presents the view that the Bible (the King James Version translated from the Masoretic and Received Texts) gives a complete, unbroken chronology of the years from the creation of Adam to the Death of Christ on the Cross. There are no gaps. The Bible and the Bible alone gives the complete chronology of the years from the First Adam to the Last Adam (I Corinthians 15:45). The Bible is not dependent in any way upon secular chronology to "fill in" any supposed gaps.

FOREWORD

> The above may be taken for granted among Bible believers, but the actual case is in fact substantially different. The standard Bible chronology followed for many generations presupposes a gap in the Biblical Record of about 90 years and seeks to fill that gap by resorting to secular history. This supposed gap lies at the beginning of the famous Seventy Weeks of Daniel. By following the "conventional wisdom" of standard chronology this great portion in the Book of Daniel is dislodged from its place as the primary cornerstone of history, chronology and prophecy.[1]

I personally trust Dr. Moorman. I have published or read most of his scholarly works and I have never found a problem.

Dr. Chris Sherbrune said:

> Virtually the only historical evidence for a BC Greek Old Testament called the "Septuagint" (= seventy man or seventy day translation, depending on the legend followed) is "The Letter of Aristeas" found in a highly spurious, non-canonical collection of writings called "The Forgotten Books of Eden." The Zondervan Preface to their Septuagint call Aristeas a "fable." The Encyclopedia of Religion and Ethics (p. 308) calls it a "manifest forgery." Notable Old Testament scholar Paul Kahle calls Aristeas "propaganda." Internally there are many factual errors in "Aristeas," such as: "Demetrious was never the royal librarian, and

---

[1] J. A. Moorman, Bible Chronology, The Two Great Divides, A Defense of the Unbroken Biblical Chronology from Adam to Christ., 2010, The Old Paths Publications, Inc. Cleveland, GA., pp. 5-6.

THE CHARACTER OF GOD'S WORDS IS NOT IN THE "LXX"

he died long before Alexandria's naval Victory..." (Thackeray, THE LETTER OF ARISTEAS). The letter tells of a conversation between Demetrious and Theodektes, but Theodektes died before Demetrius was born, and the letter itself is [tentatively] dated some 200 years later than the supposed 300 BC translation of the Old Testament into Greek, (The International Standard bible Encyclopedia, p. 2924.[2]

So why is this disparity found concerning the LXX and the Masoretic Text? I suspect it is the continued angst in certain quarters against the King James Bible, which was so disdained by Catholicism in the 17th century and following. (Perhaps one day this author will publish his book in the hopper on the history of the King James Bible). The penchant to keep the precise Words of God or accurate and faithful translations out of the hands of the man in the pew continues to this hour.

Here is allegedly a picture of the false Aristeas letter obtained from Biblioteca Apostolica Vaticana, 11th century:

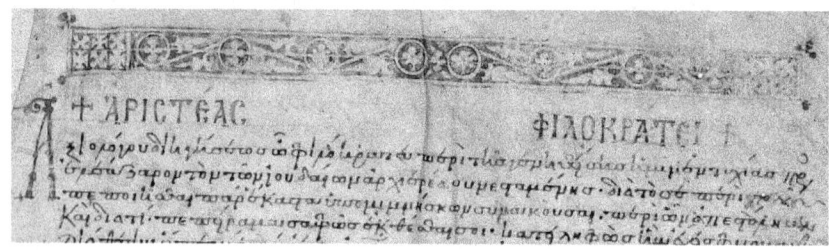

It supposedly says,

---

[2] Chris Sherburne, <u>Enough</u>, 2013, Armored Sheep Press, www.armoredsheep.com

FOREWORD

"King Ptolemy once gathered 72 Elders. He placed them in 72 chambers, each of them in a separate one, without revealing to them why they were summoned. He entered each one's room and said" "Write for me the Torah of Moshe, your teacher." God put it in the heart of each one to translate identically as all the other did (Babylonian Talmud, Tractate Megillah 9a)

After reading this work, perhaps you will conclude as I have that so much of this farce is false and shameful.

H. D. Williams, M.D., Ph. D., President
The Old Paths Publications, Inc.
www.theoldpathspublications.com
TOP@theoldpathspublications.com

TABLE OF CONTENTS

FOREWORD 5
TABLE OF CONTENTS 10
ABBREVIATIONS USED 11
THE CHARACTER OF GOD'S WORDS 14
THE INTRODUCTION 15
AN AGENDA: FABLES RATHER THAN TABLES 18
THE IMAGINARY SEPTUAGINT 22
THE CHARACTER OF THE SEPTUAGINT 25
THE IMAGINARY SEPTUAGINT USED FOR RECONSTRUCTION: . 31
WHOSE DICTIONARY AND WORDS CAN WE TRUST? 35
WHICH TEXT IS INSPIRED AND PRESERVED, THE LXX OR THE RECEIVED TEXT? 38
THE "RECEIVED" GREEK AND HEBREW TEXTS ARE SET ASIDE: REVISIONS ARE CLAIMED TO JUSTIFY FURTHER REVISIONS 43
THE DEBUNKED CANONS OF MODERNISTIC TEXTUAL CRITICS
.... 52
DID JESUS AND THE APOSTLES QUOTE THE SEPTUAGINT? 54
SO, WHAT IS THE GREEK TEXT OF THE OLD TESTAMENT? 66
THE AGENDA CONCLUDED: 75
THE CHARACTER OF GOD'S WORDS 81
THE EVIDENCE OF THE CHARACTER OF GOD'S WORDS 87
CONCLUSION 92
APPENDICES 96
BIBLIOGRAPHY 106
ABOUT THE AUTHOR 109

ABBREVIATIONS USED

A = Codex Alexandrinus

A.D. = Anno Dei

Apographs = copies of the original manuscripts

Autographs = original manuscripts

B = Codex Vaticanus

B.C. = Before Christ

ca. = circa

Canon = "In ecclesiastical affairs, a law, or rule of doctrine or discipline, enacted by a council and confirmed by the sovereign; a decision of matters in religion, or a regulation of policy or discipline, by a general or provincial council." Way of Life Encyclopedia

D.D.S. = Dead Sea Scrolls

e.g. = Latin for "exempli gratia" = for example

etc. = Latin for "et cetera" = and so forth

G = International Standard Bible Encyclopedia, Septuagint, Name, Section II, "The "Septuagint" and the abbreviated form "LXX" have been the usual designations hitherto, but, as these are based on a now discredited legend, they are coming to be replaced by "the Old Testament in Greek," or "the Alexandrian version" with the abbreviation "G,"" standing for Greek.

GTO = Greek Text of Origen

Hellenistic = Pertaining to the Hellenists. The Hellenistic language was Greek spoken or used by the Jews who lived in Egypt and other countries, where the Greek language prevailed.

Hexapla = Hex'aplar = *Gr. six; and to unfold.* Sextuple; containing six columns; from Hexapla, the work of Origen, or

THE CHARACTER OF GOD'S WORDS IS NOT IN THE "LXX"

an edition of the Bible, containing the original Hebrew, and several Greek versions.

i.e. = Latin for "id est" = "that is"

ibid = Latin for "ibidem" = "in the same place"

Inerrant = containing no mistakes

ISBE = International Standard Bible Encyclopedia

KJB = King James Bible

Lectionaries = a book containing portions of Scripture

Lego = small colored blocks of various sizes and shapes used for construction

Letter = Letter of Aristeas

LXX = Septuagint

MSS = manuscripts

MT = Hebrew Masoretic Text

NT = New Testament

Op.cit. = Latin for "opera citato" = "in the work previously cited"

OT = Old Testament

p., pp = page or pages

Plenary = full, complete, entire

Qumran = Area in Palestine 10 miles south of Jericho, Qumran was on a "dead-end street" and provided a perfect location for the isolationist sect of the Essenes to live.

Rabbinical = Rabbin, A title assumed by the Jewish doctors, signifying master or lord. This title is not conferred by authority but assumed or allowed by courtesy to learned men. Rabbinical is Latin pertaining to the Rabbins, or to their opinions learning and language.

ABBREVIATIONS

Revision = re-examination for correction; as the revision of a book or writing or of a proof sheet; a revision of statutes.

RT = Received Text

TR = Textus Receptus

TT = Traditional Text

Type = a "sign; a symbol; a figure of something to come; as, Abraham's sacrifice and the paschal lamb, were types of Christ. To this word is opposed antitype. Christ, in this case, is the antitype." (From Webster's 1868 Dictionary)

Vid. Supra = Latin for "vide supra" = See above or other material in this work

Viz = Latin for "videlicet" = namely

Vorlage = is defined by the books, Invitation to the Septuagint and Canon Debate, as the "parent text from which it is translated."

THE CHARACTER OF GOD'S WORDS

IS NOT FOUND IN THE "G"[3]

BUT IN THE ANCIENT LANDMARKS

Ps. xlv. (xlvi.) 1 – 3.

SYMMACHUS.	LXX.	THEODOTION.
ἐπινίκιος·	εἰς τὸ τέλος·	τῷ νικοποιῷ*.
τῶν υἱῶν Κόρε	ὑπὲρ τῶν υἱῶν* Κόρε	τοῖς υἱοῖς Κόρε
ὑπὲρ τῶν αἰωνίων	ὑπὲρ τῶν κρυφίων	ὑπὲρ τῶν κρυφίων
ᾠδή.	ψαλμός.	ᾠδή*.
ὁ θεὸς ἡμῶν	ὁ θεὸς ἡμῶν †	ὁ θεὸς ἡμῶν
πεποίθησις καὶ ἰσχύς,	καταφυγὴ καὶ δύναμις,	καταφυγὴ καὶ δύναμις,
βοήθεια	βοηθὸς	βοηθὸς
ἐν θλίψεσιν	ἐν θλίψεσι	ἐν θλίψεσιν
εὑρισκόμενος σφόδρα.	ταῖς εὑρούσαις ἡμᾶς ‡ σφόδρα.	εὑρέθη † σφόδρα.
διὰ τοῦτο	διὰ τοῦτο	διὰ τοῦτο
οὐ φοβηθησόμεθα	οὐ φοβηθησόμεθα	οὐ φοβηθησόμεθα
ἐν τῷ * συγχεῖσθαι	ἐν τῷ ταράσσεσθαι	ἐν τῷ ταράσσεσθαι
γῆν	τὴν γῆν	τὴν γῆν
καὶ κλίνεσθαι	καὶ μετατίθεσθαι	καὶ σαλεύεσθαι ǀ
ὄρη	ὄρη	ὄρη
ἐν καρδίᾳ	ἐν καρδίᾳ	ἐν καρδίᾳ
θαλασσῶν.	θαλασσῶν.	θαλασσῶν.
* MS. ταῖς.	* With interlinear variant τοῖς υἱοῖς (Th.). † MS. 1ª manu ἡμῶν (? Aq. Sym.). ‡ With interlinear variant εὑρεθήσεται ἡμῶν.	* With marginal variants, εἰς τὸ τέλος, ψαλμῶν (LXX.). † With interlinear variant ταῖς εὑρούσαις ἡμᾶς (LXX). ‡ With interlinear variant μετατίθεσθαι (LXX.).

A PAGE FROM ORIGIN'S HEXAPLA
NOTE THE "LXX" OVER THE CENTER COLUMN[4]

---

[3] International Standard Bible Encyclopedia, Septuagint, Name, Section II, "The "Septuagint" and the abbreviated form "LXX" have been the usual designations hitherto, but, as these are based on a now discredited legend, they are coming to be replaced by "the Old Testament in Greek," or "the Alexandrian version" with the abbreviation "G"."

[4] Henry Barclay Swete, D.D., Old Testament in Greek (Wipf and Stock Publishers, Eugene, Oregon, Originally published in 1902, Reprint, 2003) p. 62-63

THE INTRODUCTION

The character of God's words is *not* found in the "so-called" Septuagint (LXX). God's words are verbally and plenarily inerrant, infallible, inspired, preserved, and *precise* (specific). Their precision is to the jot and tittle, the smallest parts of Hebrew letters. [Mat. 5:17-18]. The LXX is not precise (specific) by any stretch of the imagination, as this document will demonstrate.

In addition, believers in the Lord Jesus Christ are to be *precisely* obedient. Our need to be *precisely* obedient rests in our love for our Saviour and for His words, which are like a legal document [Mat. 19:17; Lk. 8:15, 11:28; **Jn 12:47-48**; 14:15, 23; 15:10; 1 Cor. 15:2;1 Jn. 5:2].

A clear example of the precise commands and obedience that God desires from His followers is in the book of Joshua. However, before giving the example, we must understand or review some typology (types)[5] given in the Old Testament. In Genesis 6:14 Noah is commanded to build a *wooden* ark covered with pitch. The ark of *wood* is a type of Christ who carries us across the "storm" of life to new beginnings. The pitch represents the blood shed for us by the Lamb of God; and there is no redemption from sin without the shedding of blood which covers our sins [Jn. 1:29; Rom. 4:7; Col. 1:14; Heb. 9:22]. In Exo. 2:3 the baby Moses is placed into an ark covered with pitch and made from bulrushes.[6] The ark covered with pitch, the type of the Lord Jesus Christ, was for the baby's protection. In Deut. 10:3 Moses made an "ark of

---

[5] Type is a "sign; a symbol; a figure of something to come; as, Abraham's sacrifice and the paschal lamb, were types of Christ. To this word is opposed antitype. Christ, in this case, is the antitype." (From Webster's 1868 Dictionary)

[6] Bulrushes were used for making writing materials as wood is made into paper. The eternal son of God was begotten in an earthen vessel, made of "wood," earthly materials (Hebrews 10:5, 10). Jesus, the Word, [Jn 1:1-2] is the ultimate 'writing' instrument of God.

wood" and placed within it the two *stone* tables with the Ten Commandments. The tables had the *precise* words of God written upon them. The words had "jots and tittles" and vowel pointings. In other words, if the Hebrew Words did not have the markings, then the Hebrew consonants in the ten commandment words would be nonsensical.[7] The 'wooden ark' built by Moses now had the Word of God within it. Similarly, the begotten son of God, the Lord Jesus Christ, was placed into a body [Heb. 10:5], an 'earthen vessel' (*typically* a 'wooden' vessel), which was broken for us [Lev. 6:28, 14:50]. In His vessel, the body prepared for Him like a wooden vessel, was the Words of God that He brought, which are the *precise* words of God, the triune God, *"forever settled in Heaven"* [Psa 119:89]. He brought them to earth contained within the 'wooden' earthly vessel. That vessel was totally consumed, burnt up on the altar of the Cross for us as the perfect burnt sacrifice, that is "without blemish" (Leviticus 1:3).

The typology given to us in the book of Joshua should come to life considering the types and antitypes presented above [see footnote 3]. In Joshua 3:3-4 we discover that the Jewish nation was commanded to follow the holy "ark of the covenant" (a wooden vessel containing the words of God, typically the Holy Lord Jesus Christ) in a *precise* way. They were to **follow** the ark "about two thousand cubits by measure: come not near unto it" (v. 4). They were to follow it *precisely* "that ye may know the way by which ye must go: for ye have not passed this way heretofore" (v. 4). They were not to be in front of it or beside it, rather *following* it *precisely* for fear of turning "from it to the right hand or to the left, that thou mayest prosper whithersoever thou goest [Jos. 1:7, Psa 1].

---

[7] Dr. Thomas Strouse, *"Scholarly Myths Perpetuated on Rejecting the Masoretic Text of the Old Testament," Dean Burgon Society News*, Issues 71 & 72, Dean Burgon Society, Collingswood, NJ, 08108) 1-8. Furthermore, over 1000 Hebrew manuscripts have been discovered with the vowel pointings. The well-known commentator, John Gill, also affirms that the vowel pointings were present in the beginning. See Dr. Strouse's article.

INTRODUCTION

In light of the typology, we are to typically follow *precisely* the Lord Jesus Christ's "jots and tittles."

But that is not all the typology we need to consider. After crossing the "Jordan River" by faith and by **following precisely** the words of God, the "reproach of Egypt"[8] was removed from Israel [Jos. 5:9b, Psa. 119:22, 39]. At this point in their journey, the nation had finally learned obedience. Subsequently, the *army* of God could go **before** the "ark of the covenant" as the 7 priests carrying 7 trumpets marched around Jericho for 7 days, and on the 7th day, they marched around the city 7 times. [Jos. 6:6-15]. For a while, the nation of Israel practiced obedience to precise words without murmuring and complaining. Our sanctification should lead us to a similar place. That is, go out with or before the Words of God, carrying that precious, precise message of salvation, that is:

> He that goeth forth and weepeth, bearing precious seed, shall doubtless come again with rejoicing, bringing his sheaves with him. **Ps 126:6**

How can one follow or use a document, such as the LXX, that is corrupt, that does not contain precision, nor is it based upon precision, and whose history is based on fables? One purpose of this paper is to explore the duplicity associated with the Septuagint. We are in God's army and for us to be allowed to go **before** the "Ark of the Covenant," we must be precise [Mat. 5:17-18, 24:35; Jn. 12:47-48, 14:15; Jos. 3:3-4, 6:6-15; 2 Tim. 2:1-4].

---

[8] The constraints of space do not allow this author to pursue the typology of the Jordan River and Egypt, but please accept that the Jordan River is typical of surrendering or yielding to the Lord Jesus Christ, and that Egypt is a type of the lost sinner in the world.

AN AGENDA: FABLES RATHER THAN TABLES

The "common" method of examining the history of the Greek text of the Bible by students, 'scholars', teachers, and authors is to consider the **_legendary_** Greek translations of the **Old Testament** texts called the *Septuagint*[9] (abbreviated LXX), supposedly written by unknown translators, at unknown places, and at *an* unknown time. This system focuses the hearer's attention on mythological stories *immediately*, which are subsequently attributed some veracity by those heralding the stories, which will be explained. The Apostles Peter and Paul warn us about *"fables"*[10] and about *"vain jangling"* (babble), *"which some having swerved have turned aside"* to mythological stories from the truth and to nonstop **_possibilities_** (e.g., nonstop "genealogies" of descendants or of texts). The questions raised are great fodder for never-ending conjecture; and there are many who try to **force** "new" revelation or truth from the *speculation*. The frequently repeated possibilities become truth in the mind of the storytellers and hearers; and the reality that they are only fabrications that minister "endless" questions, possibilities, suppositions, conjectures, theories, guesses, speculations, or hypotheses is soon forgotten. [1 Tim 1:4, 6; 4:7; 2 Tim 4:4; Tit. 1:14; 2 Pe 1:16]. As a result, the *"**mythological Septuagint,**"*[11] the OT Greek Translation, becomes a reality in the minds of many individuals, when in

---

[9] The first use of the Latin term, Septuagint (meaning 70, therefore LXX), was by Augustine of Hippo (354-430 A.D.) following the *Letter of Aristeas* fable which referred to *hebdomekonta presbyterio* (70 elders). Eusebius of Caesarea (263-339) referred to it as *para tous hebdomekonta*, Josephus (37/38-100 A.D.), Origin (250), Philo (20 B.C.-50 A. D.) and Epiphanius of Salamis (315-403 A. D.) refer to it. See pp. 70-74 of the Canon Debate cited below.

[10] Greek, muthoi from which we get myths

[11] Dr. Gary E LaMore, *"Keep Rank...Can You?"* (Paper presented to the DBS Annual Meeting, Heritage Baptist University, 2004) p. 17.

THE AGENDA: FABLES RATHER THAN TABLES

truth it does not exist.[12] What is the ***agenda*** of those perpetuating the fable and the fraud? Behind every fraud is an agenda. The purpose of this paper is to look briefly at the agenda, the history, the text, and the duplicity associated with the "G," standing for the Old Testament Greek text, which is commonly known as the LXX or Septuagint.

The following ***example* of *fraud*** is given to demonstrate that fraud is associated with an agenda. It is not presented as a theological issue. It is a less well-known *example* of a deception demonstrating a hidden agenda, which is like the Septuagint fable and is often repeated in the classrooms and in literature. It concerns the history of the *first* Baptist church planted in America. Dr. Bill Grady has documented that not only is the date of 1638 for the establishment of the *first* Baptist church at Providence, Rhode Island deceptive, but the person credited with *establishing* the *first* Baptist church in America is not the one who founded it.

Roger Williams did ***not*** establish the *first* Baptist church in American in 1638. Rather, he established a pseudo-church in 1639 at Providence. Dr. John Clark, a physician from England and a true Baptist (Roger Williams was not a true Baptist), was the founder of the *first* Baptist church in Newport, Rhode Island in 1638. Dr. Grady concludes:

> Thus we may confidently conclude that the first *church at Newport* and *not* the first church at Providence, is the *true* first Baptist church in America, and *Dr. Clarke,* and *not* Roger Williams, was the founder and pastor of the *first* Baptist church in Rhode Island and America![13]

---

[12] Floyd Jones, Th.D., Ph.D., The Septuagint, A Critical Analysis (KingsWord Press, Woodlands, TX, 6th edition) p. 3-9, 19-21.

[13] William P. Grady, Th.D., Ph.D, How Satan Turned America Against God (Grady Publications, Knoxville, TN, 2005) p. 113 [see pages 103-121 for the full story].

THE CHARACTER OF GOD'S WORDS IS NOT IN THE "LXX"

What is the agenda of those perpetuating the false information? According to Dr. Grady, the *scheme* of those corrupting the *first* Baptist church history in America is based upon launching support for pedobaptism. Roger Williams was a pedobaptist who immediately baptized 11 (eleven) other pedobaptists into his "church." Dr. Grady states:

> "This ruse of the devil was orchestrated for a *specific* purpose indeed. With the Providence congregation designated the "first Baptist church in America," pedobaptists have been able to....challenge the legitimacy of all subsequent Baptist growth,"[14]

Here is another well-known *example* of fraudulent scholarship with an agenda. Many of you reading or hearing this paper were taught the counterfeit *critical* Greek text in Bible college or seminary. The *critical* text was *constructed* from unsupported, baseless, *critical* text canons and with much deceit (see below). The agenda was and is to destroy the *authority* of the Received Traditional Texts (the Received Greek and Masoretic Texts), which are the inspired, preserved inerrant text that God promised He would keep (see Greek **τηρέω = tAreo** or Hebrew שָׁמַר = shamar and נָצַר =natsar.) There is an *agenda* or scheme in many plans that is based on deceit and half-truths. To think otherwise is to be naïve.

Most of us have been innocently duped somewhere along the path of our lives. However, when institutions or individuals continue to declare fraudulent documents and their documentation as useful (e.g., *The Letter of Aristeas)*, especially when contrary evidence proves there is foolishness involved, it exposes three potential issues:

---

[14] Ibid. Grady, p. 103.

THE AGENDA: FABLES RATHER THAN TABLES

1. There is a plan (agenda)
2. There is pride.
3. There is deception.

> *The fear of the LORD is to hate evil: pride, and arrogancy, and the evil way, and the froward mouth, do I hate. [Proverbs 8:13]* [forward = Heb. tahpukah = fraud, deceit HDW]

Why does God hate these things? God hates them because these things lead innocents astray.[15] The author of this paper innocently used a "bible" for many years that was *constructed* from corrupted texts promoted by academic messengers from around the world who had an agenda or were duped as so many were in regard to the texts of Scripture.

> *"[B]ut I obtained mercy because I did it ignorantly in unbelief. And the grace of our Lord was exceeding abundant with faith and love which is in Christ Jesus." [1 Tim. 1:13b-14]*

There is an agenda related to the Septuagint. The "evil" of the corrupted Septuagint is persistently promoted through "pride and arrogancy." The following information exposes the agenda and folly associated with the "so-called" Septuagint, or LXX, or "G." The history and information related to the Septuagint is an affront to the *character* (see below) of God and to the Words of God.

---

[15] Exo. 23:7, Psa 15:5, Psa 19:13 are about abuse of the innocent. Many individuals are responsible for the "shedding of innocent blood" for which they will be held accountable. Leading innocent man astray by fraud may well cause their souls to be lost (their blood to be shed) for eternity. [Psa 94:21, Isa 59:7] Was this Judas' great sin? [Mat. 27:4]

THE IMAGINARY SEPTUAGINT

There are many myths associated with an Old Testament Greek translation and its origin. Most of these fables focus on an infamous "book"[16] called the "*Letter of Aristeas*"[17] (hereafter called the *Letter*) and the alleged claims of the *Letter's* documentation by authors who wrote before the first coming of our Lord Jesus Christ and in the first few centuries following His first sojourn on earth.[18] The only extant *Letter is* dated from the eleventh century! In addition, there is no pre-Christian Greek translation of the Hebrew Old Testament text, which the *Letter* alleges, that has been found, including the texts among the Dead Sea Scrolls. It is suspected that there may have been a ***local*** Alexandrian translation of a **few** of the Old Testament books by the time of Christ. However, most Jews did not respect it, except those in Egypt, because it was such an idiomatic collection of patchwork translations of some of the books of the OT.[19]

Moreover, speculations persist about the value of the *Letter*. However, Albert C. Sundberg, Jr., writes:

> The Letter of Aristeas, however, **proved to be a fiction**.[20] [my emphasis, HDW]

---

[16] Lee Martin McDonald and James A. Sanders, Editors, Canon Debate (Hendrickson Publishers, Peabody, MA, 2002). Josephus, Jewish Antiquities, *12.100, Aritaiou biblion* cited, p. 70

[17] The *Letter* is "preserved in the supposedly Lost Books of the Bible, See footnote five, p. 3, in Jones, Floyd, Th.D., Ph.D., The Septuagint, A Critical Analysis, KingsWord Press, Woodlands, TX, 6th edition,

[18] Jones, Floyd, Th.D., Ph.D., The Septuagint, A Critical Analysis, KingsWord Press, Woodlands, TX, 6th edition, p. 5;

[19] DiVietro, Dr. K.D., Did Jesus & the Apostles Quote the Septuagint (LXX)?, The Bible for Today, Collingswood, NJ, B.F.T. # 2707, p. 4

[20] Lee Martin McDonald and James A. Sanders, Editors, op. cit., p. 74.

However, Sundberg joins with others to promote the fictional document reporting,

> "Swete and Thackeray suggest that, despite Hody's devastating critique of the *Letter of Aristeas*, there still remained a kernel of historical material."[21]

Karen Jobes and Moises Silva in their book, <u>Invitation to the Septuagint,</u> released in the year 2000 relate:

> Even though the authenticity of the letter *should be rejected*, some of its information is <u>probably</u> reliable.[22] [my emphasis, HDW]

Probably?
    Sundberg, quoted above, goes on to explain that the reason for believing there is some historical truth in the *Letter* is that in the *Letter* are recorded two instances, which he concludes are significant. Two individuals, dating ca. 380 B.C., using

> "the translations of the Law," which is "of divine origin" (i.e. from the Hebrew) for "plays" either developed "cataracts in both eyes" or "was driven out of his mind."[23]

In other words, the translations were terrible. From the paucity of information presented, no one could conclude that a translation of the Old Testament or the Pentateuch, the first five books of the OT, was available. [i.e. perhaps only the sections of the Hebrew text, for the "plays," were translated

---

[21] Ibid. p. 76
[22] Karen H. Jobes and Moises Silva, <u>Invitation To The Septuagint</u> (Baker Academic, Grand Rapids, MI, 2000) p. 34.
[23] Ibid. p. 75.

from "the Law."] Furthermore, these fabulous "instances" articulate exaggerations, superstitions, fables, and vain jangling. Men develop "cataracts" and go "out of their mind" while doing many things in life. However, anywhere the *Letter* is presented or discussed, exaggerations soon appear.

In addition, not only is the *Letter* "fictional," but Dr. Moises Silva and Dr. Karen Jobes in their book, <u>Invitation to the Septuagint</u>, agreed that the purpose of the *Letter* to establish a pre-Christian "Septuagint" is **hyperbole** (exaggeration) and state:

> "Strictly speaking, there is **<u>no such thing</u>** as the Septuagint. This may seem like an odd statement in a book entitled *Invitation to the Septuagint,* but unless the reader appreciates the fluidity and ambiguity of the term, he or she will quickly become confused by the literature."[24] [my emphasis, HDW]

And in another place in their book, they state:

> "The reader is cautioned, therefore, that there is **<u>really no such thing</u>** as *the* Septuagint."[25] [emphasis mine, HDW]

---

[24] Karen H. Jobes and Moses Silva, op. cit., p. 30.
[25] Ibid, p. 32.

THE CHARACTER OF THE SEPTUAGINT

Not only is there no such thing as a *Septuagint,* but what is presented as the text of the LXX or "G" is a mess. Dr. Waite, a linguist, states:

> It can be clearly seen...that the Septuagint is <u>inaccurate</u> and <u>inadequate</u> and <u>deficient</u> as a translation. To try to reconstruct the Hebrew Text (as many connected with the modern versions are attempting to do) from such <u>loose</u> and <u>unacceptable</u> translation would be like trying to reconstruct the Greek New Testament from the Living Bible of Ken Taylor."[26] [my emphasis, HDW]

In addition, Dr. J. A. Moorman, a manuscript expert and a DBS member, states:

> "The Greek of the LXX is not straightforward Koine Greek. ***At its most idiomatic***, it abounds with Hebraisms; at its worse it is little more than Hebrew in disguise. But with these reservations the Pentateuch can be classified as fairly idiomatic and consistent, though there are traces of it being the work of more than one translator. Outside the Pentateuch some books, it seems, were divided between two translators working simultaneously, while others were translated piecemeal at different times by different men using widely different methods and vocabulary. Consequently the style varies

---

[26] Dr. Jack Moorman, <u>Forever Settled</u> (The Dean Burgon Society Press; Collingswood, NJ, 1999) p. 14-15.

THE CHARACTER OF GOD'S WORDS IS NOT IN THE "LXX"

from fairly good Koine Greek (as part of Joshua) to indifferent Greek (as in Chronicles, Psalms, the Minor Prophets, Jeremiah, Ezekiel, and parts of Kings) to literal and **sometimes unintelligible translation** (as in Judges, Ruth, Song of Solomon, Lamentations, and other parts of Kings).

Thus the Pentateuch is generally well done, though it occasionally paraphrases anthropomorphisms offensive to Alexandrian Jews, **disregards consistency in religious technical terms**, and shows its impatience with the repetitive descriptions in Exodus by **mistakes**, **abbreviations**, and **wholesale omissions**...Isaiah as a translation is bad; Esther, Job, and Proverbs are free paraphrases. The original LXX version of Job was much shorter than the Hebrew; it was subsequently filled in with interpretations from Theodotin...and the original LXX rendering is nowadays to be found in only two MSS and the Syriac..."[27] [my emphasis, HDW]

Dr. Waite in his book, <u>Defending the King James Bible</u>, comments on the *Septuagint*:

I have written a study on that based upon Dr. Charles Fred Lincoln's notes which he taught us when I was a student at the OLD Dallas Theological Seminary. [B.F.T. #9] He taught us a course on "Covenants and Dispensations." He quoted Berosis, and Martin Anstey *The Romance of Bible Chronology*. Dr. Lincoln taught us that the Masoretic text of Genesis 5 and 10 is accurate and ***the Septuagint text is not* [accurate]**. The first question is: Can you

---

[27] Moorman, op. cit., p. 14-15.

use the genealogies in Genesis 5 and 10? Can they be used as chronological data? We say yes. The second question is: Which text do you use, the Septuagint text or the Masoretic Hebrew text? Well, we take the Masoretic Hebrew text. The Septuagint text, instead of 4004 B. C. lists about 2000 more years--you get about 6004 B. C. The Septuagint adds extra years. The years are not the same.[28] [my emphasis and addition, HDW]

Drs. Silva and Jobes also state:

"We have **no evidence** that any Greek version of the Hebrew Bible, or even of the Pentateuch, was called the Septuagint" ***prior to*** the second century of this era. [my emphasis, HDW]

Dr. Robert Barnett, Vice-President, Dean Burgon Society (DBS), in his address, *Francis Turretin on the Holy Scriptures*, to the DBS in 1995 indicated Francis Turretin's opinion:

"FOURTEENTH QUESTION: THE SEPTUAGINT -- Is the Septuagint version of the Old Testament authentic? We deny."[29]

Dr. Gary LaMore wrote a paper, *"...Keep Rank...Can You?,* concerning slippage of institutions and individuals away from the KJB and the Received Texts. In that paper he states:

---

[28] Pastor. D. A. Waite, Th.D., Ph.D., Defending the King James Bible (Bible For Today, Collingswood, NJ, 4th Printing, 1992) p. 229.
[29] Dr. Robert Barnett, *"Septuagint,"* (*DBS Message Book,* Bible For Today, Collingswood, N.J., 1995) 1-4

THE CHARACTER OF GOD'S WORDS IS NOT IN THE "LXX"

"...the [**so-called**] *Septuagint sometimes has a reading that appears older or closer to what scholars think was the original text of the Hebrew Bible and can form the basis of an emendation (a correction of a text that **seems** to have been corrupted in transmission).[30] [my underlined emphasis]

The <u>Way Of Life Encyclopedia</u> reports,

"But the Septuagint (LXX) version for the most part is worse than a Living Version. It is the Old Testament written in Greek. **It is rotten**. **Its text is corrupt**. Even the *International Standard Bible Encyclopedia* (ISBE) article on the Septuagint (LXX) states that it has a **_very tattered and inferior Greek text_**. Remember, the ISBE is no friend of the King James Bible's text. The use of the Septuagint (LXX) by these new versions instead of using the Hebrew text is a serious error."[31] [my emphasis, HDW]

Since Dr. Silva and Jobes rightly conclude that there is "no such thing as the *Septuagint*" (vid. supra) and they also rightly conclude;

"The term Septuagint, which has been used in a **_confusing variety of ways_**, gives the **_inaccurate_** impression that this document is a homogeneous unit."[32] [my emphasis, HDW]

---

[30] LaMore, op. cit., p. 17.
[31] David Cloud, <u>Way of Life Encyclopedia</u> (Way of Life Literature, Port Huron, MI, 2002) p. 335.
[32] *Op. cit.* Jobes and Silva, p. 29.

THE CHARACTER OF THE SEPTUAGINT

They continue on the following pages to outline the use of the name, *Septuagint*,

"to refer to several quite different things."[33]

They conclude that perhaps the name refers to the following:

1. "Any and all ancient Greek translations of the Hebrew Bible."
2. "A particular printed edition of the Greek text" where either Old Testament or Old Testament and New Testament are meant.
3. A particular printed edition of a "reconstructed text."[34]
4. The Sinaiticus Manuscript
5. The Vaticanus Manuscript
6. The oldest Greek translation of the Old Testament *from* subsequent translations and revisions.
7. Only the oldest translation of the Pentateuch
8. The oldest translation of the Pentateuch and the rest of the Old Testament also known as the LXX/OG (OG means translations of the rest of the Bible called Old Greek)

From the mouths of these experts and those quoted below, we may safely conclude:

1. There is no such thing as the *Septuagint*.
2. The text of the *Septuagint* is a "confusing variety" of texts.
3. The text of the *Septuagint* is "corrupted," "inadequate," "inaccurate," and "rotten"
4. The text of the *Septuagint* is filled with "mistakes," "abbreviations," and "wholesale omissions."
5. The "authenticity" of the *Septuagint* is "denied."

---

[33] Ibid. p. 30
[34] Ibid. p.30

THE CHARACTER OF GOD'S WORDS IS NOT IN THE "LXX"

6. The *Letter of Aristeas* allegedly documenting the *Septuagint* is *fraudulent.*
7. There is an *agenda* related to the *Septuagint.*

Therefore, scholars, students, teachers, and anyone interested in the history of the text of Scripture should reject:

1. The use of the *Septuagint, (LXX),*
2. The name, *Septuagint (LXX)*
3. The consideration of the *Septuagint (LXX),*

for the reasons to follow. However, and most importantly, whenever the name is used, we are in a sense lending credibility or credence to an imaginary text built upon an imaginary name and a fraudulent *Letter,* which lends support to the agenda of those who **reject** the preserved, plenary, infallible, inerrant, received Words of God.

THE IMAGINARY SEPTUAGINT USED FOR RECONSTRUCTION

Furthermore, it has been demonstrated that not only has there been great **confusion** surrounding the non-entity, the imaginary Septuagint (LXX), but also there has been great **fraud** (vid. supra). This comes not only from well-trained believers in the preservation of the Words of God, but from the camp of modernistic textual critics as well, as seen above, and as will be confirmed below. In addition, as we shall see, scholars report the *construction* of Greek texts by apostate men, whether claiming to be Jews or Christians, whose texts are called the *Septuagint (LXX)*.

Yet, despite this well-known information, eminent men continue to claim the ability to *reconstruct* the Hebrew text from "the LXX" Greek texts. They claim they can use:

1. The mythological *Septuagint* Old Testament translation, **once it is found** or
2. Translations of the Hebrew text into Greek by *known* apostates called the *Septuagint by* the Ebonite's Aquila, or Symmachus, or Theodotin, etc) or
3. Poorly constructed Greek texts, or
4. Partial texts (the "short" texts of Biblical books found at Qumran, like Metzger's Readers Digest Bible), or
5. Texts with omissions, commissions, and confusion beyond comprehension (e.g. Vaticanus and Sinaiticus MSS).

DUPLICITY

The modernists claim these very poor manuscripts give significant evidence for the *reconstruction* of the *vorlage,* the parent text.³⁵ Such is the state of scholarship in these last days. (viz.) The state of scholarship today is "duplicity."³⁶

For example, Jobes and Silva, who know and understand the information presented above and below demonstrate duplicity when they state:

> "In theory, the Septuagint should allow scholars to **_reconstruct_** that earlier Hebrew text, though in practice this activity is fraught with difficulties."³⁷ [my emphasis, HDW]

If one does not know the original text being sought nor the validity of the text used for the "reconstruction," how can the text be restored? This is like a child trying to *reconstruct* a lego house without knowing the initial design. The *perfect* reconstruction of a complicated, detailed church interior as shown in the Lego pictures in the appendix without the original details would be impossible. Although liberals know and understand that there is no such thing as the Septuagint, and that the *translations* of the Old Testament into Greek are replete with "a very tattered and inferior Greek text" (e.g., many scattered Lego pieces, the "jots and tittles), they press toward "the impossible dream" and, I might add, "the unnecessary dream," wasting time and money.

We have **copies** [apographs] of the original Hebrew, Aramaic, and Greek texts [autographs], which are the

---

³⁵ Vorlage is defined by the books, <u>Invitation to the Septuagint and Canon Debate</u>, as the "parent text from which it is translated."

³⁶ <u>Webster 1828</u>: duplicity-- Doubleness of heart or speech; the act or practice of exhibiting a different or contrary conduct, or uttering different or contrary sentiments, at different times, in relation to the same thing; or the act of dissembling ones real opinions for the purpose of concealing them and misleading persons in the conversation and intercourse of life; double-dealing; dissimulation; deceit.

³⁷ *Op. cit.* Jobes and Silva, p.21.

preserved inspired Words, just as God said He would keep them for us.

The Greek *translations* of the Old Testament Hebrew and the corrupted Greek manuscripts of the New Testament such as the Aleph and B manuscripts, are a mess.[38] Yet Jobes and Silva press on and quote Albert Pietersma, who says:

> "The primary focus in LXX text-criticism must always remain on the **reconstruction** of the original text."[39] [my emphasis]

Edward Glenny, Central Baptist Theological Seminary, made a similar statement. He is obviously drinking from the same cup as the modernists or liberal critics. He said:

> "Our purpose at Central is "to ***reconstruct*** from all the witnesses available to us the text essentially preserved in all, but perfectly preserved in none" [footnote 3, Rene Pache, The Inspiration and Authority of Scripture (Chicago: Moody Press, 1969), 197]. It is evident from the historical evidence that God has providentially preserved **His Word** for the present generation. However, we do **not** believe that God has preserved **His Word** perfectly and miraculously in any one manuscript or group of manuscripts, or in all the manuscripts. Therefore, in our study of the text we work with all the manuscripts to compile a text closer to the original than any one

---

[38] David L. Brown, The Indestructible Book, (The Old Paths Publications, Cleveland, GA, 2015) pp. 112-116.

[39] Ibid. p. 124 (Jobes).

manuscript or group of manuscripts."[40] [my emphasis, HDW, notice he does not say words]

And Jobes and Silva would be so bold as to state:

"No New Testament scholar can afford to ignore the Septuagint."[41]

---

[40] Edward Glenny affirms Michael A. Grisanti, editor, <u>The Bible Version Debate: The perspective of Central Baptist Theological Seminary</u>, p. 131.

[41] Op. Cit. (Jobes) p. 24

WHOSE DICTIONARY AND WORDS CAN WE TRUST?

Why not IGNORE the *Septuagint*? It's a mess.[42] Why don't we rely on the great translation, the KJB, translated by linguists who **knew** *all* the early Greek *Christian* masters' works? Why don't we quit trying to be pseudo-scholars, forever questioning the well-documented and superior translation by superior scholars? We should stop using corrupted lexicons and manuscripts (e.g. Septuagint revisions and recensions by the dozens) written by unbelieving scholars. How can we trust Greek words used by the apostate Origen, (who was also a mental case because he castrated himself based upon Matthew 19:12).[43] to translate the Hebrew Old Testament and to help with understanding the theology of the Bible?

Most of us have been made aware of the built-in dictionary within the Bible. Dr. Floyd Jones says:

> "Moreover, context is the decisive factor for determining the final connotation of any word or phrase, not the dictionary or etymology. Etymology, though helpful, is not an exact science. It should be used for confirmation, not as the deciding factor."[44]

---

[42] This author is aware of the claim that the Septuagint acts like a theological thought bridge between the Old Testament and the New Testament as "a commentary and word study." See Dr. K. D. DiVietro, *Did Jesus & the Apostles Quote the Septuagint (LXX)* (Bible For Today, Collingswood, NJ) p. 7, and Jobes, Karen H. and Silva, Moises, *Invitation To The Septuagint* (Baker Academic, Grand Rapids, MI, 2000) p. 24-25.

[43] H.D. Williams, The Lie That Changed the Modern World, (The Old Paths Publications, Cleveland, GA, 2004) p. 50.

[44] Op. Cit. Jones, p. 36

THE CHARACTER OF GOD'S WORDS IS NOT IN THE "LXX"

This author would add to this statement that any extra-Biblical dictionary or lexicon should be used with GREAT caution. God provided His lexicon and dictionary within the words He preserved.

Although we do not agree with everything written in the book, <u>In Awe of Thy Word, Understanding the King James Bible</u> by Gail Riplinger, the documentation of the built in dictionary/lexicon in the KJB is significant; and we should take notice.[45] She states that:

> using tools from the new field of computational linguistics. This new research demonstrates what Auburn University Professor, Ward Allen calls – "[T]he miraculous perfection of the Authorized Version"[46]

The 1200 page book proceeds to document the dictionary, lexicon, alliteration, rhyme, consonance, assonance, eye-rhyme, sense rhyme, slant rhyme, echo techniques, parallel sounds and thoughts., rhythm (iambic, trochaic, anapestic, dactylic), and much more that is found in the King James Bible. [See the appendix, p. 46, for a few examples]

Furthermore, many expert students of God's words have documented that the KJB is **based** upon the **original inspired** Hebrew, Aramaic, and Greek words that are preserved for us by the Jewish scribes and the church [Rom. 3:2, 1 Tim 3:14-15]. Dr. D. A. Waite, who has a doctorate in theology and a doctorate in linguistics states:

---

[45] G. A. Riplinger, <u>In Awe of thy Word</u> (A.V. Publications Corp., Ararat, VA, 2003) a 1200 page work, which documents the built-in lexicon of the KJB. However, this author cannot accept the inspiration, "theopneustos," of the KJB.

[46] G. A. Riplinger, op. cit., p. 6.

In fact, **it is my own personal conviction and belief, after studying this subject since 1971, that the WORDS of the received Greek and Masoretic Hebrew texts that underlie the KING JAMES BIBLE are the very WORDS which God has PRESERVED down through the centuries, being the exact WORDS of the ORIGINALS themselves.** As such, I believe the are the INSPIRED WORDS. I believe they are PRESERVED WORDS. I believe they are INERRANT WORDS. I believe they are INFALLIBLE WORDS. This is why I believe so strongly that any valid translation MUST be based upon these original texts, and these alone! [All emphases in the quote were made by Dr. Waite][47]

---

[47] Dr. Harry E. Carr, Th.D. Ph.D., This I Believe, A Study in Systematic Theology (Morris Publishing, Kearney, NE, Revised 2004) p. 11.

WHICH TEXT IS INSPIRED AND PRESERVED, THE LXX OR THE RECEIVED TEXT?

Has everyone noticed the latest statements by modernistic textual critics affirming the preservation of the Words of God? Although duplicity is in their works, they confirm the preservation of the Masoretic Text. For example, Dr. Randall Price, a graduate of Dallas Theological Seminary, an expert in the Dead Sea Scrolls, states:

> "The number of Old Testament manuscripts discovered among the Dead Sea scrolls (about 223-233) is more than twice the number of New Testament Greek papyri (96). However, despite this abundance of ancient witnesses to the text of the Bible, few English translations of the Old Testament have been affected. **The reason is that generally the biblical Qumran texts are so close to the Hebrew text behind the Masoretic Text that they lend support to, rather than emend, those versions that rely upon the Received Text.**[48] [my emphasis, HDW]

The Masoretic Text **is** the very preserved words of God as He promised. In addition, the historical character of the Greek New Testament is above reproach.

> It can no longer be successfully argued that events and beliefs described in the New

---

[48] Dr. Randall Price, <u>Secrets of the Dead Sea Scrolls</u> (Harvest House Publishers, Eugene, Oregon, 1996) p. 146.

WHICH TEXT IS INSPIRED AND PRESERVED?

Testament were a product of Christian theologians centuries later.[49]

Dr. Price also counters scholars such as Bart Erhman[50] who denigrates the preserved text by stating:

> Rather than support the recent theories of documentary disunity, the Scrolls have returned scholars to a time when the Bible's internal witness to its own consistency and veracity was fully accepted by its adherents.[51]

Repeatedly, *theories*, such as a *"revision"* of the Hebrew canon at the Council of Jamnia (a.k.a. Yavneh) by Rabbinic scholars, the validity of "lost Scriptures", and false "Scriptures," are eventually discarded as fraudulent.[52]

However, despite the information gleaned concerning the preservation and inspiration of the words of God, duplicity raises its ugly head when Dr. Price states:

> To properly understand this concern we must distinguish between inspiration and preservation. Inspiration refers to the original autographs [Hope he is referring to the ***process*** of inspiration, Gr. **Θεόπνευστος** = theopneustos, and not the materials written upon. The inspired words are preserved in apographs. HDW] of the Bible as given by God through men, while preservation has to do with

---

[49] Ibid. p. 140 . (Price).

[50] Bart Ehrman, Lost Christianities (Oxford University Press, New York, NY, 2003) also see Lost Scriptures, by the same author and publisher.

[51] Price, op. cit., p. 164.

[52] *Canon Debate,* op. cit., p. 91, 146-62.

THE CHARACTER OF GOD'S WORDS IS NOT IN THE "LXX"

copies that have been passed down through the ages by human agency alone. Some people confuse preservation with inspiration and contend that the copies that have come down to us cannot have been altered in any way from the autograph, such as in an English translation like the King James Version. [This is idea is Ruckmanism. See below, HDW] This erroneous view must be rejected as both unbiblical and unfactual. Nothing in biblical statements such as "All Scripture is inspired by God" (2 Timothy 3:16), "Until heaven and earth pass away, not the smallest letter or stroke shall pass away from the Law, until all is accomplished" (Matthew 5:18). Or Heaven and earth will pass away, but My words will not pass away" (Mark 13:31) requires that every inspired word must likewise be preserved *outside* of the autographs. [This is vintage B. Warfield. Yes He did say He would preserve them, Psa. 12:6-7, 1 Pr. 1:25, or He is a liar, which He is not. Titus 1:2 HDW] Yet we *can* say—and say with greater confidence than ever based on the witness of the Scrolls—that our present text is accurate and reliable, and that nothing affecting the doctrine of the original has been compromised or changed in any way in the manuscript copies. The Scrolls have affirmed that the Masoretic Text behind our English translations *was* carefully preserved.[53] [my comments, HDW]

Dr. D.A. Waite, Dr. T. Strouse, Dr. J. Moorman and others have repeatedly attested to the truth that the words accurately copied from the autographs are just as inspired as the original words. God did not promise to preserve the

---

[53] Price, op. cit., p. 145.

materials the words were written upon, but the words. Those words preserved in the ***virtually*** identical Received manuscripts (apographs) are the inspired words of God in the Hebrew, Aramaic, and Greek texts.

For example, Dr. Waite has reported this certainty in over 20 places in many of his works. Here are two samples and a complete list is appended to this work.

> " I have never said that the King James Bible is a perfect translation. This would be the Dr. Peter Ruckman view. He uses the words inerrant, and infallible when referring to the English. **I use those terms inerrant and infallible to refer to the original autographs and to the Hebrew and Greek texts which God has preserved for us today. Those are inspired Words in the Hebrew. Those are inspired words in the Greek. Since God has preserved those Hebrew and Greek words I believe by faith that those Hebrew and Greek words are inerrant and infallible.**"[54]

In another work, Dr. Waite says,

> "Let's be very careful about this. It is true that the process of inspiration applies only to the autographs and resulted in inspired Words the original Words of Hebrew, Aramaic, and Greek being given by God's process of breathing out His Words. The process has never been repeated; the manuscripts that we have today were not the result of the process of inspiration. **However, it can be said that the Words given originally by the process of**

---

[54] Dr. D. A. Waite, PhD. ThD., Central Seminary Refuted on Bible Versions (Bible For Today, Collingswood, NJ) p. 42.

<u>**inspiration if they have been preserved exactly in manuscripts we have today are inspired Words. If, then, they are the same Words that God gave by the process of inspiration, we can refer to them as inspired Words. To say it another way, I believe that words in the apographs (the copies of the original manuscripts) that are accurate copies of the original Hebrew, Aramaic, and Greek words can be referred to as inspired Words. In this sense, therefore, (since they have been preserved Word for Word) I refer to the Hebrew and Greek Words that underlie the King James Bible as inspired Words.**</u> This is a major point that needs to be kept clear."[55]

---

[55] Dr. D. A. Waite, PhD. ThD. <u>Fundamentalist Mis-Information on Bible Versions</u> (Bible For Today, Collingswood, NJ) p. 58.

THE "RECEIVED" GREEK AND HEBREW TEXTS ARE SET ASIDE: REVISIONS ARE CLAIMED TO JUSTIFY FURTHER REVISIONS

Yet, most liberals or modernists subtly denigrate the Received Greek and Masoretic Texts as a basis for pursuing the (imaginary) Septuagint by repeating the chant from the modernist's camp concerning the theories of a Lucian or Syrian "recension" of the Greek text *and* a revision of the Hebrew text. They frequently refer to the Lucian or Syrian theory as fact and call it the time when the text was "standardized (see http://www.textusreceptusbibles.com/Editorial/LucianRecension)."[56]

> "Although the transmission of the Greek NT was stabilized as early as the fourth century, leading to its *standardization* [i.e. reconstructed or recension, HDW] in a form known as the Byzantine Text,"[57] [my emphasis, HDW]

There is no evidence for a Received Text "standardization" (recension) during the third or fourth century. This is another oft-repeated **supposition** without any validity or evidence. Dean Burgon calls it

> "the (imaginary) Syrian Revision of A.D. 250 and A.D. 350,"

---

[56] One reason they may have started using "standardization" is to subtly undermine the name some believing Bible students use for the Received Greek and Hebrew text, "the standard text."

[57] Jobes and Silva, op. cit., p. 147.

and he goes on to state:

> Drs. Westcott and Hort require us to believe that the authors...interpolated the genuine text of the Gospels with between 2877 (B) and 3455 (Aleph) spurious words; mutilated the genuine text in respect of between 536 (B) and 829 (Aleph) words, substituted for as many genuine Words, between 935 (B) and 1114 (Aleph) uninspired words., licentiously transposed between 2098 (B) and 2299 (Aleph); and in respect to number, case, mood, tense, person, etc. altered without authority between 1132 (B) and 1265 (Aleph) words.[58]

What we do have are many copies of the Received Text from many countries and verified in many different languages; and we have many Received Text *verses* from many church fathers' quotes.[59] Wilbur Pickering believed a reading should be attested to by a wide variety of witnesses meaning

> "in the first place, many geographical areas, but also different kinds of witnesses—MSS, Fathers, Versions, and Lectionaries."[60]

He said Burgon addressed the idea of variety in regard to both aspects, saying:

---

[58] H. D. Williams, M.D., Ph.D., The Lie That Changed the Modern World (The Old Paths Publications, Inc.; 2004) p. 209.

[59] Dr. Jack Moorman, Early Manuscripts, Church Fathers, and the Authorized Version (The Old Paths Publications, Inc., 2005).

[60] Wilbur Pickering, Th.D., The Identity of the New Testament Text (Thomas Nelson Publishers, Nashville, TN, 1980) p. 142.

THE RECEIVED GREEK & HEBREW TEXTS SET ASIDE

"Variety distinguishing witness massed together must needs constitute a most powerful argument for believing such Evidence to be true. Witnesses of different kinds; from different countries; speaking different tongues:--witnesses who can never have met, and between whom it is incredible that there should exist collusion of any kind:--such witnesses deserve to be listened to most respectfully. Indeed, when witnesses of so varied a sort agree in large numbers, they must needs be accounted worthy of even implicit confidence... Variety it is which imparts virtue to mere Number, prevents the witness-box from being filled with packed deponents, ensures genuine testimony. False witness is thus detected and condemned, because it agrees not with the rest. Variety is the consent of independent witnesses,...

It is precisely this consideration which constrains us to pay supreme attention to the combined testimony of the Unicials and of the whole body of the Cursive Copies. They are (a) dotted over at least 1000 years: (b) they evidently belong to so many divers countries,--Greece, Constantinople, Asia Minor, Palestine, Syria, Alexandria, and other part of Africa, not to say Sicily, Southern Italy, Gaul, England and Ireland: (c) they exhibit so many strange characteristics and peculiar sympathies: (d) they so clearly represent countless families of MSS., being in no single instance absolutely identical in their text, and certainly not being copies of any other Codex in existence,--that their unanimous decision I hold to be an absolutely irrefragable evidence of the Truth."[61]

Dean Burgon was talking about the Received Text (Textus Receptus). Dr. Waite says:

"If you are talking about the Textus Receptus of the New Testament we find those manuscripts **virtually identical** one with the other...a seamless garment. There are a few spelling differences but other than that not much else."[62]

The *Hebrew* (Received) Masoretic Text is also "put out to pasture" by the similar claim of reconstruction. They use the Dead Sea Scrolls (D.S.S.) as "evidence" of a pre-Christian Septuagint "closer to the *vorlage*." However, no B. C. **<u>Greek</u>** Old Testament text can be produced with **<u>ANY</u>** certainty. But when it comes to the Masoretic Text, they suddenly ignore the evidence of many of the D.S.S. and claim a revision to the Hebrew text in the first century. They know that the evidence in the D.S.S. shows the mimeo-graphic like quality of several Biblical books and state the facts clearly. Yet, elsewhere in their writings, they forget this evidence and claim a revision. It also slips their minds that the cultic Essene community separated from the *orthodox* Jewish community. Israel, the Jews were given the responsibility by God to copy and preserve the text. Romans 3:2 states,

---

[61] Dean John William Burgon, <u>The Traditional Text of the Holy Gospels, Vol 1</u> (The Dean Burgon Society Press, Collingswood, NJ, 1998) pp. 50-51.
[62] Pastor D. A. Waite, Th.D., Ph.D., <u>Fuzzy Facts From Fundamentalists on Bible Versions</u> (The Bible For Today, Collingswood, NJ) p. 65.

THE RECEIVED GREEK & HEBREW TEXTS SET ASIDE

> *"Much every way: chiefly, because that unto them (the Jews), were committed the oracles of God." (My addition, HDW)*

Here are some examples affirming this duplicity.

> "The few Qumran texts that **differ** from the MT have deservedly received much *scholarly* attention."[63] [MT equals the Masoretic Hebrew Text; My emphasis, HDW]

In the same book, this statement is made:

> "It is clear from the Hebrew texts found at Qumran that the MT, is indeed an ancient text that was **already stable before** the time of Jesus."[64]

Yet this comment also is made:

> "In spite of the remarkably accurate work of the Masoretes, scribal changes prior to the **standardization** of the Hebrew text need to be identified and evaluated. The LXX is our primary source for such data, and in some biblical books it may contain a significant number of textual variants that would have been present in its parent text."[65]

Obviously, the data available to many liberal scholars today is ignored. Another significant finding in <u>Invitation to the</u>

---

[63] Jobes and Silva, op. cit., p. 176.
[64] Ibid. p. 177 (Jobes and Silva).
[65] Ibid. p. 146 (Jobes and Silva).

THE CHARACTER OF GOD'S WORDS IS NOT IN THE "LXX"

<u>Septuagint</u> is the ignoring of information concerning the nearly exact copies of several Biblical books found in the D.S.S. For example, J. P. Green reports that a copy of the book of Isaiah in the D.S.S. matches the Hebrew Masoretic Text:

> "Much more recently, at Qumran, two manuscripts of Isaiah have been found. One of them is complete, and dates from the 1st century before Christ. The surprising and amazing thing about this textual evidence, is that the 10th century A.D., Masoretic text is in substantial agreement with the text of Isaiah, that has been buried for two thousand years. **The two texts are in amazing agreement, except for a number of minor punctuation-type variations.**"[66]

In addition, Dr. T. Holland writes in <u>Crowned with Glory,</u>

> Until recently, the most ancient manuscripts of the Hebrew Old Testament dated to the ninth century. This has changed with the discovery of the Dead Sea Scrolls, which date from 168 BC to about 68 AD. The scrolls provide us with Hebrew manuscripts more ancient than the previous manuscripts by one thousand years. What is interesting to the student of textual criticism and the believer in Biblical preservation is that **the majority of Biblical manuscripts among the Dead Sea Scrolls agree with the Masoretic Text**. This further provides evidence of the text's credibility and testifies to the accuracy of the Hebrew scribes in their reproduction of biblical manuscripts throughout the ages. **Consequently, it establishes the preservation of the Old Testament text in Hebrew by God.**

---

[66] Jay P. Green, <u>Unholy Hands on the Bible, Vol. II</u> (Sovereign Grace Trust Fund, Lafayette, IN, 1992) p. 364.

THE RECEIVED GREEK & HEBREW TEXTS SET ASIDE

The earliest Biblical fragments among the Scrolls come from the book of Leviticus (1QLev.*a*) and add support to the antiquity of the Masoretic Text. These fragments encompass **Le** 19:31-34; 20:20-23. There is but one minor variant from the Masoretic Text found in **Le** 20:21. The Masoretic Text uses the Hebrew word *hoo* while the Dead Sea Scrolls uses the Hebrew word *he*. It is the same Hebrew word and is a personal pronoun meaning *he*, *she*, or *it*. The two are used interchangeably throughout the Hebrew Old Testament.

Additional manuscripts have also been found that supports the Masoretic Text. In the early 1960's Biblical texts were discovered during the excavation of Masada, the renowned rock fortress where Jewish zealots made a successful last stand against the Roman army after the destruction of Jerusalem in 70 AD. These texts were approximately nineteen hundred years old, dating slightly before 73 AD when Masada finally fell. The manuscripts were exclusively Masoretic. To these we can also add the Geniza Fragments which were discovered in 1890 at Cairo, Egypt. These fragments date to the fifth century AD. They were located in a geniza, a type of storage room for worn or faulty manuscripts. The fragments number around 200,000 and reflect Biblical texts in Hebrew, Aramaic, and Arabic. The Biblical texts discovered support the Masoretic Text.

In one sense, the Masoretic Text may be thought of as the Textus Receptus (Latin for *received text*) of the Old Testament. In fact, some scholars have referred to it as such. Like the Textus Receptus of the New Testament, the Masoretic Text is based on the majority of manuscripts and reflects the Traditional Text used. Although there are differences found in some Masoretic Texts, these differences are minor and usually deal with orthography, vowel points, accents, and divisions of the text. In 1524-25, Daniel Bomberg published an edition of the Masoretic Text based on the tradition of Jacob ben Chayyim, a Jewish refugee who later became a Christian. It was his text that was used by the translators of the *King James Version* for their work in the Old Testament. Wurthwein notes that the text of ben Chayyim was looked upon as almost canonical, and was considered the authoritative Hebrew text.[67]

In light of this information, how can Dr. R. Price (previously quoted p. 16) make the claim that God's clear statements of preservation do not "require that every inspired word must likewise be preserved outside the autographs." Liberals would rather cast doubt-producing remarks about the preservation of the Hebrew text, by making suppositions about preservation despite God's words, which cannot be proved. For example, Jobes and Silva say that prior to the alleged rabbinic "standardization" of the Hebrew text after 70 A.D. that:

> "From the time that, say, the prophecies of Isaiah were written down to the time of rabbinic standardization, more than eight centuries transpired. It is only reasonable to **assume** that competing forms of the book of Isaiah would have existed during the long stretch."[68] [my emphasis, HDW]

To the credit of Jobes and Silva, however, they do admit when discussing the short Greek version of Jeremiah compared with the longer Jeremiah text of the Masoretic Text that:

> "One must remember, however, that the conclusions offered by scholars rest on a very small sample of actual Hebrew text and a great deal on a reasonable, but nonetheless hypothetical, reconstruction."[69] And "Only by appreciating the condition of the preserved fragments and the nature of the reconstruction can one understand the tentativeness of

---

[67] Dr. Thomas Holland, <u>Crowned With Glory, The Bible from Ancient Text to Authorized Version</u> (SwordSearcher, Version 4.6, Broken Arrow, OK) Chapter 6.

[68] Jobes and Silva, op. cit., p. 148.

[69] Ibid, Jobes and Silva, p. 175.

THE RECEIVED GREEK & HEBREW TEXTS SET ASIDE

any conclusion about the relationship of 4QJer^{b,d} to the Greek Jeremiah and the MT."[70]

---

[70] Ibid, Jobes and Silva, p. 176.

THE DEBUNKED CANONS OF MODERNISTIC TEXTUAL CRITICS

In addition, Jobes and Silva are brave and/or unwise to recommend the use of the "canons" of textual critics, which are debunked by the likes of modernistic unbelieving textual critics such as Kurt Aland and K. W. Clark.[71] Those "canons" emanate from the wells of infidelity of modernistic textual critics such as Griesbach, Westcott, and Hort; and include "canons" such as "intrinsic probability," "transcriptional probability," and "genealogy." There is no such thing as "genealogy" of texts. See <u>The Lie That Changed the Modern World</u>.

Jobes and Silva recommend them in chapter 6 (the number for man in Scripture) as reliable tools for "reconstructing" the text of the Septuagint. They reinforce their recommendations with the warning:

> "the fact that canons of textual criticism are often misused leads some scholars to minimize their importance and even to suggest that they should be jettisoned. That would be a serious mistake."[72]

They quote Westcott and Hort's <u>New Testament in the Original Greek</u>, stating:

> "Knowledge of documents should precede final judgment upon readings."[73]

---

[71] Williams, op. cit., pp. 191-196, 215.
[72] Jobes and Silva, op. cit., p. 129.
[73] Ibid. p. 132 (Jobes and Silva).

Surely they must know that Westcott and Hort knew very little about the history or genealogy of "documents" because they never did the genealogical studies. **They lied.**[74]

---

[74] Williams, op. cit., pp. 191-194.

DID JESUS AND THE APOSTLES QUOTE THE SEPTUAGINT?

Jobes, Silva and many other liberals conclude in several passages in Invitation to the Septuagint that Jesus and the apostles quoted the "so-called" Septuagint. For example, they state:

> "the New Testament writers sometimes used expressions found in the Septuagint to draw the readers mind to specific passages of Old Testament Scripture...Clearly Paul is using vocabulary from the Greek version of Isaiah 45:23...Third, the New Testament writers frequently quote the Greek Old Testament directly—*perhaps* as many as three hundred times."[75]

And they quote Richard N. Longenecker, saying:

> "the citations by Jesus "are strongly Septuagintal."[76]

Many others have chanted this refrain, ignoring sound evidence against the proposition. For example, Craig A. Evans is quoted in The Canon Debate, and said:

> "Jesus' scripture quotations and allusions sometime agree with the Septuagint against the proto-Masoretic Hebrew. Jesus' quotation of Isa

---

[75] Ibid, p. 23-24.
[76] Ibid, p. 193.

> 29:13 is quite septuagintal, both in form and meaning (cf. Mark 7:6-7)."[77]

Yet, stuck in the middle of a technical paragraph are these comments by Craig A. Evans, which demonstrate duplicity:

> "Of course, agreements with the Septuagint no longer require us to think that Jesus read or quoted the Septuagint. Thanks to the Bible scrolls of the Dead Sea region, we now know that there were Hebrew *Vorlagen* underlying much of the Greek Old Testament."[78]

There is no requirement at all, and not only that, there is **NO** evidence that Jesus or the Apostles quoted the Septuagint. Furthermore, we have the Masoretic text, which is the inspired, preserved Words of God, the vorlagen that was used for the King James Bible. Dr. D. A. Waite, DBS President, Dr. Kirk D. DiVietro, Secretary of the DBS, and Dr. Floyd Jones have decisively defeated the claim that the Lord Jesus Christ quoted from the Septuagint. However, Craig goes on to say that Jesus quotations:

> "agree with some Greek versions against others."

However, his conclusion is sadly depreciating of our Lord and the preserved Scripture. Craig says:

---

[77] Lee Martin McDonald and James A. Sanders, The Canon Debate, (Hendrickson Publishers, Peabody, MA, 2002) Chapter 11 by Craig A. Evans, p. 192.
[78] Ibid. p. 192.

> "Jesus' use of the Bible attests **the diversity** of the textual tradition that now, thanks to the Scrolls, is more fully documented."[79] [my emphasis, HDW]

Apparently, Craig means that Jesus quoted from several different text types because he read and studied several different versions. Therefore, his assumption or guess justifies using the critical text (CT) and its many editions (see the UBS's many editions of the Greek text). Oh, how sad! According to Craig, the LORD and Creator of the universe had to resort to many books to determine which quote He was to use; or perhaps He left just a summary "message" from all that He had read. I am being sarcastic. Sorry, but this is so frustratin. Craig's guess would agree with Samuel Schnaiter's infamous statement:

> "With regard to preservation, however, no Scripture explicitly declares anything of this sort of guidance to apply to the manuscript copyists as far as the precise wording of the text is concerned. Some have deduced such supernatural guidance from Scripture. They note passages that promise God's Word shall never perish or be lost. However, such promises of preservation in view of **the wording variations must apply only to the message of God's Word, not its precise wording**"[80] [my emphasis, HDW]

Jesus, the Word, said,

---

[79] Ibid.

[80] Samuel Schnaiter, <u>Relevancy of Textual Criticism</u>, 1980. Bob Jones University Press, Greenville, SC.

> *Heaven and earth shall pass away, but my <u>words</u> shall not pass away. [Mat. 24:35]*

Therefore, did the Lord Jesus Christ quote the Septuagint or did he quote the Hebrew Old Testament. Dr. Waite clearly says:

> **"The Old Testament Hebrew Text Was Authorized by Jesus.** Not only was the Scripture **accumulated** by Jews, but it was **authorized** by Jesus. Jesus Christ authorized the traditional Masoretic Hebrew Old Testament text. Though we have looked at some of these verses under the subject of **Bible preservation,** we will look at them once more from a slightly different aspect.
>
> **a. Verses Teaching This Position**.
>
> **(1) Matthew 4:4**. Jesus was speaking to the devil and refuting him with Scripture:
>
> *"But He answered and said,* ***IT IS WRITTEN****, Man shall not live by bread alone, but by* ***EVERY WORD*** *that proceedeth out of the mouth of God."*
>
> As we said before, *"it is written"* is in the perfect tense, meaning it has been written in the past and stands written now, preserved until the present time. **So the Lord Jesus Christ AUTHORIZED the Old Testament He had in His hand.** The first books of the Old Testament were originally written by Moses around 1500 B.C. The Old Testament Hebrew Words were preserved for 1,500 years and the Lord Jesus said, *"it is written."* This means that the **WORDS OF GOD** have been written down in the past and these very **WORDS** have been preserved down to the present time, and they stand written NOW as they were at the first. This is the very essence of BIBLE PRESERVATION!

THE CHARACTER OF GOD'S WORDS IS NOT IN THE "LXX"

(2) Matthew 5:17-18. Jesus speaks about the *"law or the prophets."* This is a technical term referring to the traditional Masoretic Hebrew Old Testament text. There are three divisions in the Old Testament: the Law, the Prophets, and the Writings. Sometimes the expression, "law and prophets," refers to all three divisions. The Law (the *torah*) refers to the first five books; the Prophets (the *naviim*) refers to both the former and the latter Prophets; and the Writings (the *kethuvim*) refers to the Psalms and the rest of the books. Here in verses 17 and 18 Jesus said,

*"(17) Think not that I am come to destroy the **LAW**, or the **PROPHETS**: . . . (18) For verily I say unto you, Till heaven and earth pass, one **jot** or one **tittle** shall in no wise pass from the Law, till **all** be fulfilled."*

Jesus said of the words, letters, and even parts of the letters found in the Hebrew Bible in His day, that no jot or **tittle** would be eliminated, effaced, or changed in the slightest manner until all was fulfilled. So He put His **AUTHORIZATION** on the traditional Masoretic Hebrew text He had in His day.

(3) Luke 24:27. When the Lord Jesus Christ talked to the disciples on the road to Emmaus, He taught them:

*"And beginning at **Moses** and all the **prophets**, He expounded unto them the things concerning Himself."*

Here is the phrase *"**Moses and all the prophets**."* It leaves off the "writings," but again, this was referring to the threefold division of the Hebrew Bible: Law, Prophets and Writings. That is **AUTHORIZATION** by the Lord Jesus of the traditional Masoretic Old Testament Hebrew text that was present in His day.

DID JESUS AND THE APOSTLES QUOTE THE "LXX"?

(4) Luke 24:44.

*"And He said unto them, These are the words which I spake unto you, while I was yet with you, that all things must be fulfilled, which were **written** in **THE LAW** of Moses, and in **THE PROPHETS**, and in **THE PSALMS**, concerning Me."*

The Greek word *"written"* is *gegrammena*, the perfect participle: that which was written in the beginning and is continuously being preserved and stands written today. The phrase *"in the Psalms"* makes it the complete threefold division of the Hebrew canon: the law of Moses (Torah); the prophets (Naviim); and the Psalms or Writings (Kethuvim). It is called the *"TANACH"* today by the Jews, taking the *"TA"* for *"TORAH,"* the *"NA"* from *"NAVIIM,"* and the *"CH"* for *"KETHUVIM."* This is the one abbreviation for the entire Masoretic Hebrew Old Testament. **He put His hand on the entire Masoretic Hebrew Old Testament text that existed then and AUTHORIZED it.** Many people may ask, "Didn't the Lord Jesus Christ use the Septuagint Version of the Old Testament? Wasn't He referring to that?" No, he was not. He referred to the Law of Moses, the Prophets, and the Psalms. The Septuagint did not have that division at all. In fact, aside from the Apocrypha contained in the Septuagint, the order is LAW, PSALMS, and PROPHETS instead of, as the Hebrew, LAW, PROPHETS & PSALMS. As you can see, the Septuagint has the order of books much as we have in our Bibles today. The Hebrew does not have the same order; it ends with the book of 2 Chronicles.

b. Quotations Explaining This Position. Christ appealed unreservedly to the traditional Hebrew text.

(1) A Quotation from Dr. Edward Hills. Here is a quotation from Dr. Edward Hills, who has written extensively on the subject of the Bible.

THE CHARACTER OF GOD'S WORDS IS NOT IN THE "LXX"

"During His earthly life, the Lord Jesus appealed unreservedly to the very words of the Old Testament text (Matthew 22:42, John 20:44 ff), thus indicating His confidence that this text had been accurately transmitted. Not only so, but He also expressed this conviction in the strongest possible manner, `. . . till heaven and earth pass, one jot or one tittle shall in no wise pass from the law till all be fulfilled,' (Matthew 5:18.) . . . Here our Lord Jesus assures us that the Old Testament in common use among the Jews during His earthly ministry was an **ABSOLUTELY TRUSTWORTHY REPRODUCTION OF THE ORIGINAL TEXT WRITTEN BY MOSES AND OTHER . . . WRITERS."** *[BELIEVING BIBLE STUDY, by Dr. Edward Hills, pp. 5-6].*

The Lord Jesus Christ never refuted any text, any word, or any letter in the Hebrew Old Testament. He didn't say, "Now Moses was misquoted here, it should have been this." He offered no textual criticism whatever. Had there been any changes, I'm sure He would have corrected it, but He didn't. It stands written! His stamp of approval is on the Masoretic Hebrew text. It is **AUTHORIZED** by Jesus. He did not authorize the Septuagint, the Latin Vulgate, some scribal tradition, Josephus, Jerome, the Syriac version, or any other document!

(2) A Quotation from Dr. Robert Dick Wilson. Here is a quotation from Dr. Robert Dick Wilson, a Presbyterian, and a teacher at Princeton Seminary before the flood of Modernism came in. Henry Corey reflected on the life of Dr. Robert Dick Wilson, a man who had mastered some forty-five languages and dialects and who was a staunch defender of the doctrine of verbal inspiration of Scripture. Corey affirmed that Wilson accepted as **accurate** the Masoretic Hebrew text. Corey, quoting Wilson, wrote:

"The results of those 30 years' study [that is what Wilson wrote of his own study of Scripture in the Hebrew] *which I have given to the text has been this: I can affirm that there's not a page of the Old Testament in which we need have any doubt. We can be absolutely certain that substantially we have the text of the Old Testament that Christ and the Apostles had and which was in existence from the beginning."* [WHICH BIBLE, 1st edition, by Dr. David Otis Fuller, pp. 80-81].

Here is a man who studied, and studied, and found the Masoretic Hebrew text to be accurate and solid. So I see no reason why we should have any other foundation for the Old Testament than the Masoretic Hebrew text that underlies the KING JAMES BIBLE, the **Daniel Bomberg edition,** edited by **Ben Chayyim**--the **2nd Rabbinic Bible of 1524-25**.

c. Alternative to Believing This Position? You might say, what is the alternative? What if you do not accept the **Daniel Bomberg edition** of the **Masoretic Hebrew** text on which the KING JAMES BIBLE is based as the **authoritative** Hebrew text from which to translate? The alternative, quite logically, would be to accept some other basis. What other basis are you going to use? Are you going to use the Kittel *Biblia Hebraica* (**BHK**) which was based upon the same text as the KING JAMES BIBLE in 1906 and 1912, and then was revised and scrapped for another Hebrew text in 1937? Or are you going to use the 1967/77 *Biblia Hebraica Stuttgartensia* (**BHS**) which is a revised Kittel? If you're not going to use the base that is printed in the **defective** Hebrew text at the top of the page in either **BHK** or **BHS**, are you going to use some of these changes in the footnotes--20,000 to 30,000 of them? If so, which ones are you going to use? Are you going to use only the ones they used in the NEW KING JAMES VERSION? Only the ones they used in the NEW AMERICAN STANDARD VERSION? Only the ones they used in the NEW INTERNATIONAL VERSION? Are you going to use

THE CHARACTER OF GOD'S WORDS IS NOT IN THE "LXX"

25% of them? 50% of them? Or are you going to use all of them? Or are you going to become a doubter, thinking that we don't really know what the Old Testament is? Are you going to take the position that "We can't be certain of the Hebrew Old Testament, so we must doubt all of it"? **Satan is the master of deceitful doubting and he is the author of all this confusion.** Once you forsake a standard, you're adrift in a sea of doubts. There's nothing to take its place. Young Christians and people in the pews that have not been saved too many years might say, "If there's all this bickering and fighting among the theologians and pastors as to the right Hebrew Old Testament text to use, I give up and throw up my hands." The devil wins if he can plant the seeds of confusion and doubts into the hearts of men and women as well as boys and girls.

After much study, thinking, and praying about this subject, I have personally arrived at a **strong conviction** that I will not budge from the traditional Masoretic Hebrew text on which our KING JAMES BIBLE is based. That is it. I'm not going to move. I don't want to change anything. We're going to stand right there. Somebody's got to stand. **Martin Luther said, "Here I stand; I can do no other."** He wasn't going to move from salvation by faith (*sola fide*), salvation by grace (*sola gratia*) and salvation only by the Scripture (*sola scriptura*). He wasn't going to follow the Pope. He wasn't going to follow the decrees of the Church Councils. He was standing on the Word of God alone! Though we might not be Lutherans like Martin Luther, we must not budge either. If we do, we are like a wave of the sea, driven by the wind and tossed."[81]

The truth is that there is **no** pre-Christian era Septuagint (OT Greek Translation) that was allegedly translated from the Hebrew OT in Alexandria, Egypt in the third century B. C., which the Lord Jesus Christ and the apostles used. There may

---

[81] Waite, op. cit., Defending the King James Bible, p. 32-37.

be an **idiomatic** translation of a few books such as the Pentateuch, but there is no evidence of a formal equivalent translation of the Old Testament. Furthermore, Dr. Floyd Jones states unequivocally that:

> "There exists no verses that any New Testament writer quoted from any Greek manuscript written prior to 120 A.D."

Not only does he make the statement above, but also his frustration is reflected in the following statement:

> "Thus we stand perplexed and frustrated. We have examined the origins of the LXX and found them lacking, full of fable, myth, and legend. Now we stand deceived and misled, having been told that a B.C. Septuagint is available for use only to find that such an ancient document does not actually exist anywhere in the world."[82]

It is being proclaimed that a Greek text of the minor prophets found in the caves of the Judean desert is "an important link in the textual history" of the "G." However, the findings in the cave have been dated around 132-135 A. D.; and so, it could be one of the known Christian era Greek translations such as the Quinta (see below).[83]

Why don't those scholars struggling with such profound confusion surrounding the "G" (their new name for the misnomer, Septuagint) simply drop the anxiety of trying to "*reconstruct*" an *imaginary* text and discover that "his yoke is easy and [his] burden is light." Yes, some prideful positions and some "filthy lucre" may have to be abandoned, but the

---

[82] Op. Cit. Jones, p. 19.
[83] Op. Cit. Jobes and Silva, p. 171-172.

bondage to pseudo-science and pseudo-history will be relieved and the hours wasted on nonproductive labour can be turned to assisting brokenhearted people.

C. H. Spurgeon spoke about the modernists and their "duplicity" and removing *the ancient landmark.* He said:

> "We have lived to see a certain sort of men…who seek to teach, nowadays, that God is a universal Father, and that our ideas of His dealing with the impenitent as Judge, and not as a Father, are the remnants of antiquated error. Sin, according to these men, is a disorder rather than an office, an error rather than a crime. Love is the only attribute they can discern, and the full-orbed Deity they have not known. Some of these men push their way very far into the bogs and mire of **falsehood**, until they inform us that eternal punishment is ridiculed as a dream. In fact, books now appear which teach us that there is no such thing as the vicarious sacrifice of our Lord Jesus Christ. They use the word atonement, it is true: but, in regard to its meaning they have removed ***the ancient landmark***. They acknowledge that the Father has shown His great love to poor sinful man by sending His Son, but not that God was inflexibly just in the exhibition of His mercy, nor that he punished Christ on behalf of His people, nor that, indeed, God ever will punish anybody in His wrath, or that there is such a thing as justice apart from discipline. Even sin and hell are but old words employed henceforth in a new and altered sense…These are the new men whom God has sent down from Heaven to tell us that the apostle Paul was all wrong, that our faith is vain, that we have been quite mistaken, and that there was no need for propitiating blood to wash away our sins: our

sins needed discipline, but penal vengeance and righteous wrath are quite out of the question! When I thus speak, I am free to confess that such ideas are not boldly taught by a certain individual whose volume excites these remarks, but as he puffs **the books of gross perveters of the truth**, I am compelled to believe that he endorses such theology." [C.H.S. The Early Years, p. 488, O Timothy magazine, Vol. 8, Issue 1 1991] [my emphasis, HDW]

The Lord Jesus Christ and the apostles did **not** quote from the *Septuagint*. The so-called LXX quoted them, and in classic allegorist fashion, the authors changed any Greek words that did not fit their Alexandrian Gnostic and Arian philosophy (see below). [Col. 2:8]

SO, WHAT IS THE GREEK TEXT OF THE OLD TESTAMENT?

The *questions, probabilities, possibilities, problems* and *use* related to the imaginary *Septuagint* proposed by individuals such as Karen Jobes, Ph.D., Moises Silva, Ph.D., Henry Barclay Swete, D.D.,[84] Sir Lancelot C. L. Brenton,[85] and the International Standard Bible Encyclopedia (ISBE) have been answered by men in the Dean Burgon Society as well as Dean Burgon himself and by others. In addition, what is so appallingly apparent in the liberal's dialogue is the paucity of discussion of the Received or Traditional Greek and the Masoretic Text by name. They skirt the issue by glancing comments about alleged recensions of texts, but never, ever discuss the possible implications of thousands of texts (manuscripts) from many authors and many countries that are in many languages, which attest, to the preservation of the Received Text.

Dr. Kirk D. DiVietro and Dr. Floyd Jones have written two poignant astute documents, which are available from *Bible For Today* concerning the so-called *Septuagint*. They resoundingly trounce the wild *assumptions* of the modernistic *Septuagint* scholars by simple clear concise statements.

Dr. Jones makes a clear statement at the beginning of his treatise on the *Septuagint* about what is known concerning the Septuagint. He states:

> "The Septuagint (LXX) is a very old translation of the Hebrew Scriptures (our Old Testament) into Hellenistic Greek. This statement alone is

---

[84] Henry Barclay Swete, D.D.; Old Testament in Greek (Wipf and Stock Publishers, Eugene, Oregon; Originally published in 1902, 2003).

[85] Sir Lancelot C.L. Brenton, The Septuagint with Apocrypha: Greek and English (Hendrickson Publishers, Peabody, MA, originally published in 1851).

almost the *only* hard fact concerning this translation that is verifiable."[86]

The other known fact about the misnomer, *Septuagint*, is that it is a non-entity. The name is adapted from a fraudulent document, *Letter of Aristeas*. The only extant *Letter* is an eleventh century document. Today, the manuscript that is generally called the *Septuagint* is the Old Testament Greek translation constructed by Origin Adamantius, called Codex B (c.245 A.D.).[87] This is the real recension as opposed to the theoretical recensions of the Received Greek and Hebrew Texts. Codex B is the 5th (fifth) column of Origin's *Hexapla,* a six column parallel Bible. Origen labeled the 5th (fifth) column the **LXX** (See the picture on page 5 of this work). This may be observed in the fragment of the *Hexapla* by Origen found at Milan, Italy in 1896 and published in <u>An Introduction to the Old Testament in Greek</u> by Henry Barclay Swete D.D. in 1902.[88]

Dr. DiVietro says:

> "Scholars lie. In the case of the Septuagint, the lie is not as overt as usual…The Septuagint, as it is published today, is basically the text of the Old Testament as it appears in Codex B."[89]

Codex B, the LXX, is a revision of the Greek text<u>s</u> extant during Origin's time. He used the versions of the Ebonite's' Aquilla (c. 128), Symmachus (c. 180-192 A.D.), and

---

[86] Floyd Jones, Th.D. Ph.D., <u>The Septuagint: A Critical Analysis</u> (Kings Word Press, The Woodlands, TX 6th Edition, 2000) p.1.

[87] Op. Cit. Jones, p. 19

[88] Henry Barclay Swete, op. cit., pp. 62-63.

[89] Op. Cit. DiVietro, p. 2-3. Also, see Dr. Floyd Jones statement in *The Septuagint*, pp. 19, 53.

Theodotin (c. 161-181) for the *Hexapla* reconstruction,[90] along with three other anonymous translations that have become known as the Quinta, the Sexta, and Septima.[91] From this point on in this paper the OT Greek text, usually misnamed LXX or Septuagint, will be called the Greek Text of Origen, GTO. A Greek text of the minor prophets found in the Judean desert caves dates to around the time of "the second Jewish revolt in the years 132-135" A.D. by the personal letters of Bar Kokhba. They cannot be claimed with any certainty as part of a B.C. *Septuagint*. As a matter of fact, they contain translational features found in other A.D. texts such as those of Aquila and of the Quinta.[92]

There have been many *revisions* of GTO. For example, Hesychius of Alexandria (martyred c. 311 A. D.) and Lucian of Antioch, an Arian, (martyred 311) made revisions.[93] There have been dozens of revisions through the centuries. A few of the more recent revisions are "the 1587 Sixtus, Holmes-Parson, von Tischendorf (Swete, p. 187), Swete, the Brooke-McLean great Cambridge edition, and Rahlfs 1935 edition,"[94]

Jerome (340-420 A.D.), a contemporary of Augustine of Hippo, ridicules the GTO often in his letters. However, the texts he used for his translations for Rome, the Latin vulgate, were of "the Alexandrian text type."[95] And so, Jerome needs to be ridiculed for using Alexandrian texts from Alexandria, Egypt. Before reading the following quotes from Jerome's works, recall he is removed from Origin (182-251 A.D.) by over 150 years. A comparison is to imagine a student in 2005 trying to reconstruct a particular history in 1850 in America without the aid of computers, phones, extensive libraries, airplane travel, and other modern conveniences. In addition, we

---

[90] Op. Cit. Jones, p. 15-16.
[91] Op. Cit. Jobes and Silva, p. 43.
[92] Ibid. p. 171-172 (Jobes and Silva).
[93] Op. Cit. Jones, p. 17.
[94] Op. Cit. Jones, p. 51.
[95] Op. Cit. Willliams, p. 236.

must remember Jerome was opposed to the independence of local churches from Rome, represented by the Waldensians.[96] Lastly, he was obviously duped by the fraudulent *Letter of Aristeas,* which was **allegedly** commented on by the Alexandrian Aristobulus, the Neo-plantonist Philo, and the Roman historian, Josephus the Jew. They all add embellishments to the story of the *Letter.*

Dr. Phil Stringer, President, Landmark Baptist College, states:

> Jerome understood that the Septuagint of his day was developed by Origen. He believed that Origen used several different Greek manuscripts and that all of them had been corrupted! He disputed Augustine's assertion that the apostles usually quoted from the Septuagint! He pointed out that their quotations often don't match any version of the Septuagint or any other Greek New Testament.[97]

From Jerome's writings, one can quickly ascertain that Jerome is confused by the term, *Septuagint,* and denigrated it by the following quotes. Jerome says:

> "How can the Septuagint leave out the word 'Nazarene' if it is unlawful to substitute one word for another? It is sacrilege either to conceal or to set at naught a mystery."[98]

---

[96] Op. Cit. Williams, p. 237-239.

[97] Dr. Phil Stringer, *"Was the Septuagint the Bible of Christ and the Apostles?"* (*The Landmark Anchor,* Haines City, FL,Vol. 3, Issue I, May 2005) p. 7.

[98] Phillip Schaff, Translator, "The Principle Works of Jerome, Letters of Jerome." (Ages Librarian, The Nicene and Anti-Nicene Church Fathers) p. 289.

THE CHARACTER OF GOD'S WORDS IS NOT IN THE "LXX"

> Let my critics tell me why the Septuagint introduces here the words 'look thou upon me.'" "For its rendering is as follows, 'My God, my God, look thou upon me, why hast thou forsaken me.'"[99]

> It would be tedious now to enumerate, what **great additions and omissions the Septuagint has made**, and all the passages which in church-copies are marked with daggers and asterisks.[100]

> Yet the Septuagint has rightly kept its place in the churches, either because it is the first of all the versions in time, made before the coming of Christ, **or** else because it has been used by the apostles (only however in places where it does not disagree with the Hebrews).[101]

The preceding quote reveals that Jerome was duped, also. We know the Apostles did not quote from the "imaginary" (there is no solid evidence it existed before Christ) Septuagint.

> Doubtless you already possess the version from the Septuagint which many years ago **I diligently revised** for the use of students. The new testament I have restored to the authoritative form of the Greek original. For as the true text of the old testament can only be tested by a **reference to the Hebrew**, so the

---

[99] Ibid. p. 292
[100] Ibid. p. 293
[101] Ibid. p. 293

true text of the new requires for its decision an appeal to the Greek.[102] [my emphasis]

From the previous quote, we should now understand that "the LXX" is just one of the many revisions of the GTO.

> Origen, whilst in his other books he has surpassed all others, has in the Song of Songs surpassed himself. He wrote ten volumes upon it, which amount to almost twenty thousand lines, and in these he discussed, first the version of the Seventy Translators, then those of Aquila, Symmachus, and Theodotion, and lastly, a fifth version which he states that he found on the coast of Atrium, with such magnificence and fullness, that he appears to me to have realized what is said in the poem:[103]

However, no Greek "version of the Seventy Translators" has ever been found, and specifically, no Greek B.C. Song of Songs text. In addition, Jerome goes on to say:

> Add to this that Josephus, who gives the story of the Seventy Translators, reports them as translating **only** the five books of Moses; and we also acknowledge that these are more in harmony with the Hebrew than the rest.[104] [my emphasis]

Surely, the previous quote makes clear the confusion surrounding the Greek text reported by the *Letter* even during Jerome's days. Obviously, he was not sure how many, if any, of the Old Testament books had been translated. The following

---

[102] Ibid. p. 364
[103] Ibid. p. 1014
[104] Ibid. p. 1018

quote establishes that "deceitful" translators also perplexed Jerome.

> But if, since the version of the Seventy was published, and even now, when the Gospel of Christ is beaming forth, the Jewish Aquila, Symmachus, and Theodotion, **judaising heretics**, have been welcomed amongst the Greeks—heretics, who, by **their deceitful translation**, have concealed many mysteries of salvation, and yet, in the Hexapla are found in the Churches and are expounded by churchmen; [then] ought not I, a Christian, born of Christian parents, and who carry the standard of the cross on my brow, and am zealous to recover what is lost, **to correct what is corrupt**, and to disclose in pure and faithful language the mysteries of the Church, ought not I, let me, ask, much more to escape the reprobation of fastidious or malicious readers?[105] [my emphasis and addition for clarity]

Remember, Origen used the "judaising heretics" versions to make his revision, which is Codex B, the favorite corrupted text of the modernists. The next quote makes it obvious that Origen's Old Testament Greek text, composed 150 years earlier than Jerome's existence, was already being called "the Seventy."

> I have toiled to translate [and revise—see above and below, HDW] both the Greek versions of the Seventy, and the Hebrew which is the basis of my own, into Latin.[106] [In other words, Jerome made his own revision. HDW.]

---

[105] Ibid. p. 1028
[106] Ibid. p. 1028

> As, then, the Church reads Judith, Tobit, and the books of Maccabees, but does not admit them among the canonical Scriptures, so let it read these two volumes for the edification of the people, not to give authority to doctrines of the Church. If any one is better pleased with the edition of the Seventy, there it is, long since **corrected** by me. For it is not our aim in producing the new to destroy the old. And yet if our friend reads carefully, he will find that our version is the more intelligible, for it has not turned sour by being poured three times over into different vessels, but has been drawn straight from the press, and stored in a clean jar, and has thus preserved its own flavor.[107] [my emphasis] [Even Jerome rejected the apocrypha included in the GTO]

In the following quote, Jerome is not clear what he means by "descent of three steps." However, his additional comments above and below lead me to believe that he thought the three steps had corrupted "the Seventy." The comments in the middle of Jerome's quote to follow are made so that there is no ambiguity. It is interesting in the quote to follow that Jerome confirms Dean Burgon's comments concerning the "variety" of texts on p. 16

> I am not discussing the Old Testament, which was turned into Greek by the Seventy elders, and has reached us by a **descent of three steps**. I do not ask what Aquila and Symmachus think, or why Theodotion takes a middle course between the ancients and the moderns. I am willing to let that be the true translation which had apostolic approval. [In other words, even though it is "corrupted"

---

[107] Ibid. p. 1029

THE CHARACTER OF GOD'S WORDS IS NOT IN THE "LXX"

Jerome will no longer fight his adversaries, HDW]

I am now speaking of the New Testament. This was undoubtedly composed in Greek, with the exception of the work of Matthew the Apostle, who was the first to commit to writing the Gospel of Christ, and who published his work in Judaea in Hebrew characters. [This is denied. There is no evidence Matthew wrote in Hebrew. HDW] We must confess that as we have it in our language it is marked by discrepancies, and now that the stream is distributed into different channels we must go back **to the fountainhead**. I pass over those manuscripts which are associated with the names of Lucian and Hesychius,, and the authority of which is perversely maintained by a handful of disputatious persons. It is obvious that these writers could not amend anything in the Old Testament after the labors of the Seventy; and it was useless to correct the New, **for versions of Scripture which already exist in the languages of many nations show that their additions are false**. I therefore promise in this short Preface the four Gospels only, which are to be taken in the following order, Matthew, Mark, Luke, and John, as they have been revised by a comparison of the Greek manuscripts. Only early ones have been used. But to avoid any great divergences from the Latin which we are accustomed to read, I have used my pen with some restraint, and while **I have corrected** only such passages as seemed to convey a different meaning, I have allowed the rest to remain as they are.[108]

---

[108] Ibid. p. 1020-1021

THE AGENDA CONCLUDED:

So why are "scholars" spending millions of hours and millions of dollars to "reconstruct" a text from corrupted, fraudulent manuscripts, which are often written or "corrected" by unbelievers? There have been many reasons listed by various authors. The underlying spiritual reason for extolling the *possible* virtues of the GTO has not been clearly stated or has been missed. It is the old old problem recorded for us in the book of Genesis as the etiology for the fall of man. The problem is the refusal to come under *authority*. The authority of the words of God frightens men. The Apostle John record these words for us, *"Never man spake like this man,"* [Jn. 7:46] because the Lord Jesus Christ spoke **with authority**. The ultimate agenda of those promoting the LXX is to destroy the authority of God's words because "Never man spake like this man." His true words frighten men, because if they are preserved, infallible, plenary, and inerrant, they will have to come under their precise and/or specific authority and judgment. Satan and man have fought this authority "from the beginning."

If the truth about the Received Texts (Masoretic and Greek Traditional Text) can be discredited by assumptions and theories, then men can claim we have no absolute authority. Scholars are free to make up their own texts to promote their philosophies. They are free to ignore the precision (jot and tittle) and they are free from following precisely "the ark of the covenant" (see the Introduction to this work)

Dr. Phil Stringer in a recent newsletter gave an opinion why "so many 'scholars' [are] so devoted to the Septuagint." He states:

> Roman Catholics use the idea that Christ quoted the Septuagint **to justly include the apocrypha** in their Bibles. Their reasoning goes like this: 'Christ used and honored the

THE CHARACTER OF GOD'S WORDS IS NOT IN THE "LXX"

> Septuagint, the Septuagint includes the apocrypha, so Christ honored and authorized the apocrypha.' Since no Hebrew Old Testament ever included the books of the Apocrypha, the Septuagint is the only source the Catholics have for justifying their canon.[109]

The author of this paper is certain that Dr. Stringer's reason is correct. However, the underlying spiritual problem exhibited by the Catholic religion is the refusal to come under God's authority. They would rather place their (man's) tradition on equal footing (as they stated at the Council of Trent), and reject the authority of His preserved words. For anyone to claim the GTO (Origen's Greek Text) is "the word of God" considering the confusion surrounding the text, as well as the text exhibiting a very "loose," "corrupted translation" is very suspect. Dr. Stringer is correct when he states:

> "After all, if Christ did not care about the specific words of Scripture, why should we?...If Christ used the Septuagint then you can put the Bible in your own words in either a paraphrase or your own translation."[110] [specific is another word for precise, HDW]

Dr. Floyd Jones in his book asks: "Why then do conservatives uphold the LXX?" Dr. Jones' answer to his own question is (to summarize) that conservatives fear that the Received Text cannot be supported by scholarship, history, and internal proof without THE GTO.[111]

---

[109] Ibid. p. 5
[110] Ibid.
[111] Op. Cit. Jones, p. 35-37

THE AGENDA CONCLUDED

Dr. Phil Stringer in his article asks: "But why are so many evangelicals devoted to an idea for which they can not offer any proof?" Dr. Stringer's answer to his own question is:

> "Many proud evangelicals value the idea of being accepted as "scholarly" and "educated" by the world (the Catholics and the modernists).[112]

One cannot escape the reason for the fall of man even in these situations. If man cannot *receive*

> "[a]n inerrant (without error), verbal (each word), plenary (every word), inspired (God breathed, infallible (will not fail), Word of God,"[113]

as his sole authority with all its **life-giving** promises, he will be insecure and rely on man's words or "self.".

Finally, if we even use the misnomer, *Septuagint* or LXX, we are in a way affirming the existence of a document needed by the liberals to promote their theories of recensions, to allow them to "construct" a text more in line with their philosophies, and to assist them in rejecting the authority of a legal document, the words of God. Let us stop using the misnomer and give the text of Origen, principally Codex B another name, the Greek Text of Origen, the GTO.

The Scripture establishes some harsh warnings about the sanctity of the LORD's words in many ways and in many verses. For example, the LORD says near the beginning of the Scripture:

---

[112] Op. Cit. Stringer, p. 6

[113] Dr. Harry E. Carr, "This I Believe A Study in Systematic Theology," (*The Landmark Anchor*, Landmark Bible College, Haines City, FL.) p. 12.

THE CHARACTER OF GOD'S WORDS IS NOT IN THE "LXX"

> *Ye shall not add unto the word which I command you, neither shall ye diminish ought from it, that ye may keep the commandments of the Lord your God which I command you. [Deut. 4:2]*

And near the middle of the 66 books of the Bible, he says:

> *"Add thou not unto his words, lest he reprove thee, and thou be found a liar." [Proverbs 30:5-6]*

And he repeats the following well known admonition at the end of the Bible:

> *For I testify unto every man that heareth the words of the prophecy of this book, If any man shall add unto these things, God shall add unto him the plagues that are written in this book: And if any man shall **take away from** the words of the book of this prophecy, God shall **take away his part** out of the book of life, and out of the holy city, and from the things which are written in this book. [**Rev. 22:18-19**]*

I would offer for your consideration a passage in Psalm 19 below, which augments the three passages above, and adds characteristics to the *character* of the preserved words of God that are often scoffed at by most liberals and modernists.

The American Dictionary of the English Language from 1828 lists several definitions for character, which are apropos to the discussion in this work. For example:

A mark made by cutting or engraving, as on stone, metal or other hard material; hence, a mark or figure made with a pen or style, on paper, or other material used to contain writing; a letter, or figure used to form words, and communicate ideas. Characters are literal, as the letters of an alphabet; numeral, as the arithmetical figures; emblematical or symbolical, which express things or ideas; and abbreviations

and

The peculiar qualities, impressed by nature or habit on a person, which distinguish him from others; these constitute real character, and the qualities which he is supposed to possess, constitute his estimated character, or reputation. **Hence we say, a character is not formed, when the person has not acquired stable and distinctive qualities.**

and

An account, description or representation of any thing, exhibiting its qualities and the circumstances attending it;

and

The manner of writing; **the peculiar from of letters** used by a particular person. [my emphasis, HDW]

THE CHARACTER OF GOD'S WORDS IS NOT IN THE "LXX"

The Greek word, χαρακτηρ = charakter, is used in only one place in Scripture, but what a powerful place to use it. Hebrews 1:3 states:

> *"Who being the brightness of his glory, and the express image [charakter] of his person, and upholding all things by the word of his power, when he had by himself purged our sins, sat down on the right hand of the Majesty on high;*

THE CHARACTER OF GOD'S WORDS

The character of the Lord Jesus Christ's words is the "expressed image" of Him. [See the quotes from Webster's Dictionary above] Psalm 19 outlines the characteristics of God's words broken into eight "perfections" and eight "performances" of His Words. This uniqueness of His words, compared with the words of any other book in history, insures that they will accomplish His goals and will not return void. Our Lord requires that His words are not to return, "void" [Isa 55:11]. His Book is not "like any other book."

The *character* of His words is diametrically opposed to the modernistic, philosophical textual critic's belief about the character of God's words. They assume and conjecture that the Words of God need to be "reconstructed." Their proclamations exalting the subjective rules of "reconstruction" such as "intrinsic probability" and "transcriptional probability" are demolished by the insights and truths in Psalm 19 and throughout the remainder of His Book.

The liberals of today do not seem to be able to sense the reality of the preservation of His words. God said His words would endure forever [Psa. 12:6-7, Mat. 24:35, 1 Pe. 1:23-25 and many many other places]. Our prayer is that the rebellious would come under **authority**. Simply listen to His words. The old adage, "seeing is believing," is contrary to God's ways. The modern textual critic proclaims that the "evidence," which he sees in the textual history routes, is contrary to those who proclaim preservation. The words of God proclaim that hearing comes first in God's ways, not seeing. [John 9:25] The Scripture loudly declares, "faith cometh by hearing, and hearing by the word of God" [Rom 10:17]. We, who defend His preserved words, would pray that the existentialists of today's world, who proclaim that truth is "the ring of genuineness,"[114] a "feeling," a "communication with the cosmos," a "message received through a universal humanistic consciousness," or a "medium delivered legitimacy," would listen and hear God's revealed Truth.

Isaiah 55:6-9

> *Seek ye the LORD while he may be found, call ye upon him while he is near:* [7]*Let the wicked forsake his way, and the unrighteous man his thoughts: and let him return unto the LORD, and he will have mercy upon him; and to our God, for he will abundantly pardon.*
>
> [8]*For my thoughts are not your thoughts, neither are your ways my ways, saith the LORD.* [9]*For as the heavens are higher than the earth, so are my ways higher than your ways, and my thoughts than your thoughts.*

And so, ignoring these verses, the modernists ignore several important concepts such as the overwhelming evidence of the two routes in textual history. One route is like a river and wherever you sample along the river, the many samples are the same, whether it is the Received Greek, the Textus Receptus, or Hebrew Masoretic text. Speaking about the Greek Received text, Dr. Waite says it like this:

> "Erasmus at Basle simply selected manuscripts from the manuscript "river" of the traditional text (which is the text of the later Uncials, of the Cursives, of the early church fathers'

---

[114] Op. Cit. Williams, p. 211 (The Lie That Changed The Modern World). This was another canon of textual criticism used by Westcott and Hort to determine if a verse, reading, or text was the correct wording of a disputed passage. Dean Burgon made light of the principle.

quotations, and of the Lectionaries). These are the quotations and the manuscripts which he took. The Traditional Text (the Textus Receptus) is like a river; wherever you take a sample, it is virtually the same text. The stream of the Traditional Text started with the apostolic times. It's a river that runs down through history. All Erasmus did was to pick up some manuscripts from that river, all of which are basicly the same. They are *virtually identical manuscripts*—except for the Westcott and Hort type of 45 or so.

Erasmus picked up his manuscripts from Basle, Switerland. When working on his Computensian Polyglot, Cardinal Ximenez picked his up from Spain and various places. Yet the Erasmus text and the computensian Text are *virtually identical."* [my emphasis, HDW]

The second *route* is entirely different. It has small "streams" emanating from many corrupters and revisers; and only a few bad "samples" of manuscripts. The GTO, a hodgepodge of dissimilar and very limited number of old manuscripts, is the name given to the classic representations of the route characterized by rescriptus (written-over), corrupted, revised, and doctored manuscripts. The route is called a *family* to obscure the limited number of manuscripts. The modern textual critic loves to obscure these few manuscripts behind a scholarly façade of alleged textual families. When this author began studying the issue, the names of the variety of manuscripts called the LXX were perplexing. The association of the LXX with modernists' favorite manuscripts called Codex "B" Vaticanus and Codex ℵ, "Aleph," or Sinaiticus was not appreciated for several years. The reasons are now clear. *First*, the modernists' textual critic must **disconnect** the names of the manuscripts B and Aleph from the LXX to obscure the known depravity of the source texts (B and Aleph) from the GTO. *Second*, most articles, or books written about the Septuagint or the LXX by modernists, immediately confess to the confusion associated with the LXX; and therefore, the authors cannot have very poor manuscripts associated with the LXX. They would appear foolish. *Third*, In order to further hide the truth, most articles or books by modernists about Codex "B," Codex "Aleph" or similar codices, such as the Alexandrinus (A) Codex, extol the superiority of the texts with such glowing terms as "the oldest and best," and "the closest to the original." If the codices of the LXX are called the Aleph or B, they cannot obscure their extreme deficiencies, although they try by their alleged claims of the importance of Aleph and B. *Fourth*, after centuries of grappling with the LXX, everyone agrees that there is no consistency in the meaning of the LXX. In other words, does the name, LXX, refer to the Greek translation of the Old Testament, or does it refer to the Greek Old Testament and New Testament, or to the Greek Translation of the Pentateuch, the first five books of the Bible.

There is only one true, consistent *family* of manuscripts.[115] The great preponderance (99%) of the manuscripts are the Received Text (RT). The textual '*reconstructionists*' would rather throw all MSS (including the 1% of poor manuscripts) into the pot, mix them up, and pull out their "estimate" of the right words and phrases, which in reality amounts to further '*deconstructionism.*' If the textual critic would take just a moment to contemplate Satan's technique revealed in the Garden of Eden and apply it to the TWO MSS **ROUTES**, he would soon recognize that the VAST MAJORITY of the differences in the *one* family of manuscripts, called the RT, are ORTHOLOGICAL.[116] This is certainly not the case for the GTO and the texts related to the GTO.

---

[115] Moorman, op. cit., p. 67-72 *(*Forever Settled*)*.
[116] Waite, Fundamentalists Distortions.

In addition, the modernists [who reject the preserved, plenary, inerrant Scripture] ignore the evidence to follow FROM THE PRESERVED, INFALLIBLE WORDS that God has elevated His words to the highest pinnacle, to the top of all mountains, to the most important of all His creations, and to a rank above His name [Psa 138:2, KJB]. God begins His dissertation in Psa 19 with His creation of the "heavens," and He suggests to the nay-sayers that if **I** can do this, is it anything to **Me** to preserve **MY** words "from this generation forever":

Psalm 19:1-14
To the chief Musician, A Psalm of David.
*The heavens declare the glory of God; and the firmament sheweth his handywork. 2Day unto day uttereth speech, and night unto night sheweth knowledge. 3There is no speech nor language, where their voice is not heard. 4Their line is gone out through all the earth, and their words to the end of the world. In them hath he set a tabernacle for the sun, 5Which is as a bridegroom coming out of his chamber, and rejoiceth as a strong man to run a race. 6His going forth is from the end of the heaven, and his circuit unto the ends of it: and there is nothing hid from the heat thereof. 7The law of the LORD is **perfect**, converting the soul: the testimony of the LORD is **sure**, making wise the simple. 8The statutes of the LORD are **right**, rejoicing the heart: the commandment of the LORD is **pure**, enlightening the eyes. 9The fear of the LORD is **clean**, enduring **for ever**: the judgments of the LORD are **true** and*

righteous *altogether. ¹⁰More to be **desired** are they than gold, yea, than much fine gold: **sweeter** also than honey and the honeycomb. ¹¹Moreover by them is thy servant warned: and in keeping of them there is great **reward**. ¹²Who can understand his errors? cleanse thou me from secret faults. ¹³Keep back thy servant also from presumptuous sins; let them not have dominion over me: then shall I be upright, and I shall be innocent from the great transgression. ¹⁴Let the words of my mouth, and the meditation of my heart, be acceptable in thy sight, O L*ORD*, my strength, and my redeemer. [my emphasis, HDW]*

THE EVIDENCE OF THE CHARACTER OF GOD'S WORDS

God clearly says:

Psalm 138:2 [KJB] *I will worship toward thy holy temple, and praise thy name for thy lovingkindness and for thy truth: for thou hast magnified thy word **above** all thy name. [my emphasis, HDW.]*

This astounding testimony should send a shudder through the hearts of any who would question, blaspheme, cast disparaging remarks, or do harm to the work of the Trinity. Incidentally, the NIV gets this verse wrong, also. The NIV translators claim the Lord elevated His name **and** His word above all things in their translation. This translation is incorrect, as well as many other "new age" (version) translations such as the NASB. The New Living Translation is horrible. The KJB has it right. The Lord elevated His word even above His *character*. God proclaims through His servant David in this verse [Psa. 138:2] that man should:

1. *"worship toward thy holy temple,"* which is the *"pillar and ground"* of the truth [1 Tim 3:15] in this dispensation of the church and which is the temple where He dwells. The church, made up of "lively stones" [1 Pe 2:5], is to be the repository [Psa 119:11], protector, guardian, and publisher of His words.
2. *"praise thy name,"* which He has elevated to a level that is above every name [Phil 2:9].
3. *"praise thy name for thy lovingkindness,"* which is His grace and mercy [Psa 40:11].
4. *"praise thy name for thy...truth,"* which is His Son and His Words [Jn. 14:6, 17:17].

THE CHARACTER OF GOD'S WORDS IS NOT IN THE "LXX"

5. *"praise thy name...for thou hast magnified thy word above **all thy name**,"* which speaks for itself. The Hebrew word used here for "name" is שֵׁם (shem, from Strongs), used 771 times and is invariably translated name or names.

In addition, Psa 19:7-11 gives eight "PERFECTIONS" and eight "PERFORMANCES" of His words (8 is the number in Scripture for new beginnings), preceded by the acknowledgment in verses 1-6 that the creation also proclaims the mighty wonder of His words.

THE CHARACTER OF GOD'S WORDS	
THE PERFECTIONS	THE PERFORMANCES
1. **It is "perfect"** (v. 7) "perfect" = תָּמִים tamiym *taw-meem'* (literally, figuratively or morally); also (as noun) integrity, truth:-- without blemish, complete, full, perfect, sincerely (-ity), sound, without spot, undefiled, upright(-ly), whole.	1. **It "converts" the soul** (v. 7) "convert" = שׁוּב shuwb *shoob*; to turn back (hence, away) transitively or intransitively, literally or figuratively (not necessarily with the idea of return to the starting point); generally to retreat; often adverbial, again:--((break, build, circumcise, dig, do anything, do evil, feed, lay down, lie down, lodge, make, rejoice, send, take, weep)) X again, (cause to) answer (+ again), X in any case (wise), X at all, averse, bring (again, back, home again), call (to mind), carry again (back), cease, X certainly, come again (back), X consider, + continually, convert, deliver (again), + deny, draw back, fetch home again, X fro, get (oneself) (back) again, X give (again), go again (back, home), (go) out, hinder, let, (see) more, X needs, be past, X pay, pervert, pull in again, put (again, up again), recall,

THE EVIDENCE OF THE CHARACTER OF GOD'S WORDS

	recompense, recover, refresh, relieve, render (again), requite, rescue, restore, retrieve, (cause to, make to) return, reverse, reward, + say nay, send back, set again, slide back, still, X surely, take back (off), (cause to, make to) turn (again, self again, away, back, back again, backward, from, off), withdraw. <
2. It is "sure" (v. 7) "sure" = אָמַן 'aman; properly, to build up or support; to foster as a parent or nurse; figuratively to render (or be) firm or faithful, to trust or believe, to be permanent or quiet; morally to be true or certain; once (Isa. 30:21; interchangeable with 541) to go to the right hand:-- hence, assurance, believe, bring up, establish, + fail, be faithful (of long continuance, stedfast, sure, surely, trusty, verified), nurse, (-ing father), (put), trust, turn to the right.	**2. It makes the simple "wise"** (7) "wise" = חָכַם chakam, to be wise (in mind, word or act):--X exceeding, teach wisdom, be (make self, shew self) wise, deal (never so) wisely, make wiser. <
3. It is "right" (v. 8) "right" = יָשָׁר yashar straight (literally or figuratively):-- convenient, equity, Jasher, just, meet(-est), + pleased well right(-eous), straight, (most) upright(-ly, -ness).	**3. It "rejoices" the heart** (v. 8) "rejoices" = שָׂמַח samach; probably to brighten up, i.e. (figuratively) be (causatively, make) blithe or gleesome:--cheer up, be (make) glad, (have, make) joy(-ful), be (make) merry, (cause to, make to) rejoice, X very. <
4. It is "pure" (v. 8) "pure" = בַּר bar *bar* from 1305 (in its various senses); beloved; also pure, empty:--choice, clean, clear, pure.	**4. It "enlightens" the eyes** (v. 8) "enlightens" = אוֹר 'owr *ore* a primitive root; to be (causative, make) luminous (literally and metaphorically):--X break of day, glorious, kindle, (be, en-, give, show) light (-en, -ened), set on fire, shin

THE CHARACTER OF GOD'S WORDS IS NOT IN THE "LXX"

5. It is "clean" (v. 9) "clean" = טהור tahowr; pure (in a physical, chemical, ceremonial or moral sense):--clean, fair, pure(-ness).	**5. It "endures" forever.** (v. 9) "endures" עמד `amad; to stand, in various relations (literal and figurative, intransitive and transitive):--abide (behind), appoint, arise, cease, confirm, continue, dwell, be employed, endure, establish, leave, make, ordain, be (over), place, (be) present (self), raise up, remain, repair, + serve, set (forth, over, -tle, up), (make to, make to be at a, with-)stand (by, fast, firm, still, up), (be at a) stay (up), tarry. <
6. It is "true" (v. 9) "true" = אמת 'emeth; stability; (figuratively) certainty, truth, trustworthiness:--assured(-ly), establishment, faithful, right, sure, true (-ly, -th), verity.	**6. . It is "righteous"** "righteous" = צדק tsadaq; to be (causatively, make) right (in a moral or forensic sense):--cleanse, clear self, (be, do) just(-ice, -ify, -ify self), (be turn to) righteous(-ness). <
7 It is "desired" (v. 10) "desired" חמד chamad; to delight in:--beauty, greatly beloved, covet, delectable thing, (X great) delight, desire, goodly, lust, (be) pleasant (thing), precious (thing).	**7. It is sweeter than honey or the honey comb** "sweeter" = מתוק mathowq *maw-thoke'* or mathuwq {maw-thook'}; from 4985; sweet:-- sweet(-er, -ness).
8. It is "warning" "warning' = זהר zahar; to gleam; figuratively, to enlighten (by caution):--admonish, shine, teach, (give) warn(-ing). <	**8. It is "rewarding" to "keep" them** "keep" = שמר shamar, to hedge about (as with thorns), i.e. guard; generally, to protect, attend to, etc.:--beware, be circumspect, take heed (to self), keep(-er, self), mark, look narrowly, observe, preserve, regard, reserve, save (self), sure, (that lay) wait (for), watch(-man). "rewarding" = עקב `eqeb; a heel, i.e. (figuratively) the last of anything (used adverbially, for ever); also result, i.e. compensation; and so (adverb with preposition or

THE EVIDENCE OF THE CHARACTER OF GOD'S WORDS

	relatively) on account of:--X because, by, end, for, if, reward.

CONCLUSION

One of the great errors of the modernists is that they **presume** God did not or is not able to do as He proclaimed in His words.

Matthew 24:35
Heaven and earth shall pass away, but my words shall not pass away.

In order to claim that He did not preserve His words they twist the "clear and plain meaning" of His words to make them say what they presume, or surmise is true. Another way of saying this is that they practice eisegesis, which is reading into the Scripture what they want it to say. In Psa. 19:12 the psalmist declares his frustration with committing his *"errors"* saying, *"Who can understand his errors? Cleanse thou me from secret faults,"* when Gods words are clearly available and not far away. He PROCLAIMS *"the glory of God,"* [v. 1] (which in this Psalm is God's words by which He spoke into existence the creation, v. 1-6) whose words are to *"cleanse thou me from secret faults"* and to keep him from *"presumptuous"* sins. The psalmist recognizes that only **then** will he be *"upright"* and *"innocent"*. He recognizes that only **then** will *"transgressions"* not have *"dominion over me,"* and that he will be free from the great transgression of pride. In the dispensation of law, there is no forgiveness for presumptuous sins.

Many modernists claim the RT (TR) and KJB supporters are cultist, filled with pride ignoring the evidence of history. How wrong they are. We are just willing to come under *authority*, the *authority* of the preserved words of God and *defend* the preserved words, without shame or guilt. The indwelling Spirit affirms the Truth. Perhaps they should take the beam out of their eye in order to see the mote [Mat 7:4-5]

Jamieson-Fausset-Brown say in their commentary:

THE CONCLUSION

> *Or how wilt thou say to thy brother, Let me pull out the mote out of thine eye; and, behold, a beam is in thine own eye?*

We are not filled with pride; rather we humbly submit to and come under the authority of the **received words** of God [John 17:8]. We ask, "To whom do you submit? Do you submit to the reconstructed "message" of man or are you willing to submit to the preserved *legal* (allowed, permissible, authorized) document proclaimed and exalted by our Lord with all its jots and tittles?"

Matthew 4:4
> *But he answered and said, It is written, Man shall not live by bread alone, but by **every word** that proceedeth out of the mouth of God.*

John 12:47-48
> *And if any man hear **my words**, and believe not, I judge him not: for I came not to judge the world, but to save the world. ⁴⁸He that rejecteth me, and **receiveth not my words**, hath one that judgeth him: the word that I have spoken, the same shall judge him in the last day.*

Have your "received" them? There is no pride left among the "KJB" crowd.

> *"For we are not as many, which corrupt the word of God: but as of sincerity, but as of God, in the sight of God speak we in Christ."* [2 Cor. 2:17]

The KJB "crowd" has died to self and risen with the Risen Lord [Gal. 2:20] and have submitted to His will [2 Cor 4:2, 7, 10-11] as revealed in His preserved words.

1 Peter 2:24
Who his own self bare our sins in his own body on the tree, that we, being dead to sins, should live unto righteousness: by whose stripes ye were healed.

His words are "right" (cleansing) (Psa 19:8); they are a preserved legal document, preserved by the *"eyes of the Lord"* who has kept them from corruption by those who reject authority and corrupt.

Proverbs 22:12
The eyes of the LORD preserve knowledge, and he overthroweth the words of the transgressor.

Finally, we conclude like the Psalmist in verse 14 of the 19th Psalm:

Psalm 19:14
Let the words of my mouth, and the meditation of my heart, be acceptable in thy sight, O LORD, my strength, and my redeemer.

What words do you believe are *"acceptable"* in His *"sight?"* or authorized? Which words are the *"meditation"* of your *"heart?"* Are you your strength (by your reconstructed text), or can you proclaim the words of Psa 19:14?" Can you admit that if

THE CONCLUSION

*"Jesus Christ the same yesterday, and today, and for ever" [**Hebrews 13:8**]*

is true and that if Jesus is *"the Word"* [**John 1:1**] THEN THE WORD [IS] THE SAME YESTERDAY, AND TO DAY, AND FOR EVER? The Lord Jesus Christ promised this by saying:

Matthew 24:35
Heaven and earth shall pass away, but my words shall not pass away.

APPENDICES

A COMPILATION OF 21 OF DR. D. A. WAITE'S STATEMENTS CONCERNING INSPIRATION OF THE PRESERVED WORDS

#1. "In fact, it is my own personal conviction and belief, after studying this subject since 1971, that the WORDS of the Received Greek and Masoretic Hebrew texts that underlie the KING JAMES BIBLE are the very WORDS which God has PRESERVED down through the centuries, being the exact WORDS of the ORIGINALS themselves. As such, I believe they are **INSPIRED WORDS.** I believe they are PRESERVED WORDS. I believe they are INERRANT WORDS. I believe they are INFALLIBLE WORDS. This is why I believe so strongly that any valid translation MUST be based upon these original language texts, and these alone!" (Defending the KJB, around p. 47)

#2. #145 Issue: in his Figure 3-D: he mentions: "King James Version (Perfect translation?) (p. 29) " I have never said that the King James Bible is a perfect translation. This would be the Dr. Peter Ruckman view. He uses the words inerrant, and infallible when referring to the English. **I use those terms inerrant and infallible to refer to the original autographs and to the Hebrew and Greek texts which God has preserved for us today. Those are inspired Words in the Hebrew. Those are inspired words in the Greek. Since God has preserved those Hebrew and Greek words I believe by faith that those Hebrew and Greek words are inerrant and infallible.**" (p. 42 of Central Seminary Refuted on Bible Versions

#3. #271 Issue: "Did God somehow reinspire His Word . . ." (p. 56) " I do not believe that God reinspired His Word. The Words of God were God-breathed in the Hebrew text of

APPENDICES

the Old Testament with a little Aramaic. The Words of God were God-breathed in the Greek text of the New Testament. "Theo-pneustos" means God-breathed in the Greek. God did not have to reinspire His Word. That is not what I am talking about at all. The Textus Receptus is the Received Text which has been received down through the corridor of time from the apostolic age right down to the present. That does not necessitate a reinspiration. **The inspiration that was given by God (the God-breathed words of Hebrew and Greek) was a once for all inspiration. Those inspired Words have been preserved down to the present time.** Dr. Glenny does not believe that God has preserved His Words. (p. 76 of Central Seminary Refuted)

#4. #294 Issue: ". . . the false claims of anyone who says the KJV or TR is inspired . . ." (p. 62) "We have never taken the position that the Textus Receptus is inspired in the sense of the original autographs were God-breathed. The Textus Receptus was not God-breathed by a supernatural experience. **I believe the Textus Receptus that underlies King James Bible is a perfect copy of the original God-breathed autographs which God has preserved. The Words of this Textus Receptus are inspired Words because they are the exact Words of the original autographs, though not given by the process of inspiration but by copying.** The King James Bible is not God-breathed. God did not breathe out His Words in English, but in Hebrew, Greek and a little Aramaic." (p. 82, Central Seminary Refuted)

#5. "Let's be very careful about this. It is true that the process of inspiration applies only to the autographs and resulted in inspired Words the original Words of Hebrew, Aramaic, and Greek being given by God's process of breathing out His Words. The process has never been repeated; the manuscripts that we have today were not the result of the process of inspiration. **However, it can be said that the**

THE CHARACTER OF GOD'S WORDS IS NOT IN THE "LXX"

Words given originally by the process of inspiration if they have been preserved exactly in manuscripts we have today are inspired Words. If, then, they are the same Words that God gave by the process of inspiration, we can refer to them as inspired Words. To say it another way, I believe that words in the apographs (the copies of the original manuscripts) that are accurate copies of the original Hebrew, Aramaic, and Greek words can be referred to as inspired Words. In this sense, therefore, (since they have been preserved Word for Word) I refer to the Hebrew and Greek Words that underlie the King James Bible as inspired Words. This is a major point that needs to be kept clear." (p. 58, Fundamentalist Mis-Information on Bible Versions)

#6. "I agree. Copies are not "inspired in the same sense as the originals." The "originals" were given by the process of inspiration. The copies, or the apographs as we call them, were produced by the copyists. They were not given by the Holy Spirit of God as were the originals. **Once the Words were given by the process of inspiration they become "inspired words." I believe that the Textus Receptus Greek Text which underlies our King James Bible's New Testament contains "inspired Words." I believe we have "inspired Words" because I believe we have the same Words that were given by the process of inspiration in the original manuscripts (the autographs).** (pp. 110-111 of Fundamentalist Mis-Information).

#7. "**The King James Bible is the only legitimate English translation of the preserved Masoretic Hebrew text and Received Greek text which underlie it. I believe that these Hebrew and Greek texts have been "preserved" by God. As such, these Words are "inerrant," "infallible," and the very "inspired" (God-breathed) Words God first gave in the originals.** I do not believe we should use these four

APPENDICES

terms, however, concerning the King James Bible or of any other "translation." " (p. 16, Fuzzy Facts From Fundamentalists on Bible Versions)

#8. "**God has kept His promise by inerrantly, and infallibly preserving His inspired (God-breathed) Hebrew and Greek words underlying our King James Bible**." (pp. 16-17 Fuzzy Facts)

#9. "It is the only accurate English translation from its underlying preserved Words of Hebrew and Greek. **Only the original Hebrew and Greek Words and the preserved Hebrew and Greek Words underlying our King James Bible can be referred to as "inspired" or "God-breathed" Words.**" (p. 18, Fuzzy Facts)

#10. "Response #104: I don't say that the King James Bible is "given by inspiration of God," that is, "God-Breathed." I do not believe that. **The NT Greek Words underlying our King James Bible are inspired God-breathed Words. When Paul and Peter wrote them they were inspired, God-breathed Words. The exact copies of these Words are still inspired Words. I believe the preserved Masoretic Hebrew Words underlying our King James Bible are inspired, God-breathed Words."** (p. 35, Fuzzy Facts)

#11 "Response #118: **The Hebrew and the Greek Words that underlie our King James Bible are inspired Words. Since they are accurate reproductions of the inspired words they are the same inspired words that Peter, James, and Paul had written down in the copies. I do not believe that the King James Bible is "given by inspiration of God."** It is an English translation. We at the Bible For Today ministry and in our Dean Burgon Society ministry believe very strongly that the only Greek text that should be used to translate any Bible into any language of the world must be the Hebrew and Greek texts that underlie the King James Bible. The only accurate translation in the English language of the preserved Hebrew and Greek Words is the superior King James Bible." (p. 39, Fuzzy Facts)

#12. "Fuzzy Fact #129: Edward Glenny wrote: "One such proponent writes, '**It is my own personal conviction and belief after studying this subject since 1971, that the words of the Received Greek and Masoretic Hebrew texts that underlie the king James Bible are the very words which God has preserved down through the centuries, being the exact words of the originals themselves. As such, I believe they are inspired words.**'" " (p. 42, Fuzzy Facts)

#13. "Peter Ruckman believes there was a second work of inspiration which I do not believe. **I believe in the inspiration of the Hebrew and Greek words. I believe God has preserved those inspired Words in the texts which underlies our King James Bible.** He does not differentiate between my position and that of Dr. Peter Ruckman." (p. 67, Fuzzy Facts)

#14. "Response #259: I do not use the word, "inspired," ("God-breathed"--2 Timothy 3:16) when referring to the King James Bible. I do not use the word, "inerrant." I say it has no "translation mistakes." **I say that the Hebrew and Greek Texts that underlie it are preserved, inerrant, infallible, inspired, and God-breathed.** " (p. 96, Fuzzy Facts)

#15. "**Exact Copies Are "Inspired Words**" Fuzzy Fact #262: Larry Pettegrew wrote: "Neither for versions nor for manuscripts is inspiration to be claimed. Inspiration is claimed only for the primal sacred autograph." (p. 88)

16. Response #262: The "process" of inspiration, (God's breathing-out) was limited to the autographs. The

"process" does not extend to any translations or versions. However, exact copies of the manuscripts of those original Words, though not given by the "process" of inspiration, are God-breathed or inspired Words. **Because of their preservation by God, I believe that the Hebrew & Greek Words underlying our King James Bible are God-breathed or inspired Words."** (pp. 96-97, Fuzzy Facts)

17. "Inspired Copies? Quotation #13. (p. xv) Williams asked: "The question is were the copyists who copied these originals inspired? Were those copies inspired?"

Comment #13. Those who were the "copyists" of the "originals" were not "inspired." No people were "inspired" in the way the Bible uses this term. According to 2 Timothy 3:16, the words, "given by inspiration of God" translate only one Greek word, THEOPNEUSTOS. That literally means "God-breathed." God breathed out the original Hebrew, Aramaic, and Greek Words of the Bible. God did not breathe out men. He did not breathe out copyists. He did not breathe out translators or the ones who copied the originals. That would be silly. God does not breathe out people. As far as were the "copies" being "inspired," let me say this. **The "copies" were not given by the process of being "given by inspiration of God." They were given by copying. However, since those original Hebrew, Aramaic and Greek Words which were "God-breathed" are also called "inspired Words," every exact copy of those "inspired Words" can also be called "inspired Words," regardless of the date they were copied or the material on which they were copied. I am convinced and believe that the Hebrew, Aramaic, and Greek Words underlying our King James Bible are exact copies of the original Words and therefore can be referred to as "inspired Words."** Translations of those "inspired Words" must never be referred to as "God-breathed," "inspired of God," or "inspired." God "breathed-out" or "inspired" Words exclusively in the languages of Hebrew, a little Aramaic, and

THE CHARACTER OF GOD'S WORDS IS NOT IN THE "LXX"

Greek, and in no other language in the world! " (p. 12, Fundamentalist Deception on Bible Preservation)

#18. "As mentioned in #35 above, "Since "inspired" means "God-breathed" (2 Timothy 3:16), I do not believe that any translation is "inspired" or "inspired of God" or "God-breathed." **The word "inspired" (or "God-breathed") applies exclusively to the Hebrew, Aramaic, and Greek Words that underlie our King James Bible.** God did not breathe out His Words in Spanish, French, Russian, or even English. God did breathe out His Words in Hebrew, a little Aramaic, and Greek. Those are the God-breathed words." (p.29, Fundamentalist Deception)

#19. "Comment #226. No "translation" was "inspired," "inspired of God," "given by inspiration of God," or "God-breathed." **I do say that exact copies of the Words of Hebrew, Aramaic, and Greek Words are "inspired Words" because the autographs were God-breathed. The resulting Words can rightly be called "inspired" or God-breathed Words.** I differ with Bernard on this." (p. 34, Fundamentalist Deception)

#20. "**As far as the perfection of the Words underlying the King James Bible, I believe the Hebrew, Aramaic, and Greek Words underlying the King James Bible are verbally and plenarily preserved, and are inspired Words, perfect Words, inerrant Words, and infallible Words. "** (p. 110, Fundamentalist Deceptions)

#21. "Comment #312. Downey really does not know what God has said. His "Bible" is the manuscripts all over the world that he has never seen or held in his hands. We must know more than "God has spoken." What has He said? Where has He said it? **I believe God has spoken in the Hebrew, Aramaic, and Greek Words which underlie our King**

James Bible. And the King James Bible accurately translates those inerrant, inspired, verbally and plenarily preserved Words into English for all English-speaking people to know what He has said in their own language." (p. 121, Fundamentalist Deception)[117]

EXAMPLES FOR UNDERSTANDING THE BIBLE

Key Words, Word Definitions, Parallel Concepts

1. Connotation is an idea suggested by or associated with a word, e.g. the word 'Alaska' brings to mind 'cold.' (p.46)

2. Denotation indicates not what a word suggests, but what it names, e.g. Alaska is 'the most northwest state. [Isa. 28:9-10] (p. 46)

3. Use key words "by comparing their use in various places in the Bible." (p. 46)

4. "Identify words and verses which are parallel in meaning by finding their identical **surrounding** words (pegs)" (p. 46, my emphasis)

A. The definition may be the word next to the word.

B. The definition may be in the same verse.

C. The definition may be in the preceding or the following verse.

D. The definition may be somewhere in the chapter. (p. 49)

a. Example: purloining [Tit. 2:10] (p. 65-66)
b. Example: entering in [1 Thess 1:9] (p. 67)

---

[117] Any of the articles, books, and materials containing these quotes may be obtained by contacting Bible For Today, Collingswood, NJ, email: http://www.biblefortoday.org/ or phone orders Orders: 1-800-JOHN 10:9

5. Identify words and verses which are parallel (or direct opposites) in meaning by finding matching parts of speech. (p. 46)

   A. Expands definitions

   B. Expands understanding (p. 70)

     a. Example: The masculine gender of the Godhead as opposed to the neuter gender of the New age movement. [1 Jn. 1:3, 6] (p. 71

     b. Example: Walk in the light or dance in the light with Shirley MacLaine.

[Jn. 1:3, 6] (p. 71)

     c. Example: What is "these things" in 1 Jn. 2:1. Compare 1 Jn 2:1, 7 and 1 Jn. 2:3, 5 for parallel words and parts of speech to discover "these things" means "word." (p. 73)

     d. Example: Predestinated is "not who should be saved but how" and is "purposed" us to be saved **in Christ.** [See Eph. 1:3-11]. "God predestined the means of salvation" (p. 81-82)

     e. Example: The Rock the church is built upon is Jesus Christ, not Peter. [(Rock) Mat. 16:18, 1 Cor. 10:4, 2 Sam. 22:2, Ps. 18:2, 31:3, 42:9, (upon) Mat. 7:24, 26:10, 27:30, Mk 13:3, (this) Mat. 3:17, 8:27, 12:23-25, etc.] (p. 83-84

(These were from Riplinger's book, "In Awe of Thy Word." She has been discredited by many in recent years, but these principles are still valid.)

LEGO CONSTRUCTED CHURCH ILLUSTRATING TYPOLOGICALLY THE COMPLEXITY OF GOD'S WORDS (See this work, p. 14)

Using this simple similitude, one can quickly understand that to "reconstruct" this complex lego church without the original plan would be ridiculous. Similarly, the attempt to "reconstruct" the Words of God is preposterous, since we do not have the originals, but we do have the preserved Words.

APPENDICES

BIBLIOGRAPHY

Barnett, Dr. Robert, *Septuagint*, DBS Message Book, 1995, Collingswood, NJ, Bible For Today Press.

Brown, David L., Ph.D., The Indestructible Book, 2005 Cleveland, GA, The Old Paths Publications, Inc.

Burgon, Dean John William Burgon, The Traditional Text of the Holy Gospels, Vol. 1, 1998, Collingswood, NJ, The Dean Burgon Society Press.

Carr, Dr. Harry E., Th.D., Ph.D., This I Believe, A Study in Systematic Theology, Revised 2004, Kearney, NE, Morris Publishing.

Cloud, David, Way of Life Encyclopedia, Port Huron, MI, 2002, Way of Life Literature.

DiVietro, Dr. K. D, Did Jesus & the Apostles Quote the Septuagint (LXX)?, Collingswood, NJ, The Bible for Today Press.

Ehrman, Bart, Lost Christianities, New York, NY, Oxford University Press.

Ehrman, Bart, Lost Scriptures, New York, NY, Oxford University Press.

Glenny, Edward, The Bible Version Debate: The Perspective of Central Baptist Theological Seminar.

Grisanti, Michael A. editor, The Bible Version Debate: The perspective of Central Baptist Theological Seminary

Grady, Th.D., Ph.D., How Satan Turned America Against God, Knoxville, TN, 2005, Grady Publications.

Green, Jay P., Unholy Hands on the Bible, Vol II, 1992, Lafayette, IN, Sovereign Grace Trust Fund.

BIBLIOGRAPHY

Holland, Dr. Thomas, Crowned With Glory, The Bible from Ancient Text to Authorized Version, Broken Arrow, OK, SwordSearcher.

Jobes, Karen H. and Silva, Moises, Invitation To The Septuagint, Grand Rapids, MI, Baker Academic.

Jones, Th.D., Ph.D. Floyd, The Septuagint, A Critical Analysis, 6th Edition, Woodlands, TX KingsWord Press.

LaMore, Dr. Gary E., *"Keep Rank...Can You?"* (Paper presented to the DBS Annual Meeting, 2004) Collingswood, NJ, Dean Burgon Society Publishers.

Moorman, Dr. Jack, Forever Settled, Collingswood, NJ, July 1999, The Dean Burgon society Press.

Moorman, Dr. Jack, Early Manuscripts, Church Fathers, and the Authorized Version, Cleveland, GA, 2005, The Old Paths Publications, Inc.

Moorman, J. A., Bible Chronology, The Two Great Divides, A Defense of the Unbroken Biblical Chronology from Adam to Christ., 2010, Cleveland, GA, The Old Paths Publications, Inc..

Pickering, Wilbur, Th.D., The Identity of the New Testament Text, 1980, Nashville, TN, Thomas Nelson Publishers.

Price, Randall, Secrets of the Dead Sea Scrolls, 1996, Eugene, Oregon, Harvest House Publishers.

Riplinger, G.A., In Awe of thy Word, 2003, Ararat, VA, A. V. Publications Corp.

Sanders, James A. and McDonald, Lee Martin, Editors, Canon Debate. 2002, Peabody, MA, Hendrickson Publishers.

Schaff, Phillip, The Principle Works of Jerome, Letters of Jerome, The Nicene and Anti-Nicene Church Fathers, Translator, Ages Librarian Electronic

Schnaiter, Samuel, Relevancy of Textual Criticism, 1980, Greenville, SC, Bob Jones University Press.

Sherburne, Chris, *Enough*, 2013, Armored Sheep Press, www.armoredsheep.com.

Stringer, Dr. Phil, *Was the Septuagint the Bible of Christ and the Apostles,* Vol. 3 Issue 1, May, 2005, Haines City, FL.

Strouse, Dr. Thomas, *"Scholarly Myths Perpetuated on Rejecting the Masoretic Text of the Old Testament" Dean Burgon Society News*, Issues 71 & 72, Collingswood, NJ, Dean Burgon Society.

Swete, D.D., Henry Barclay, Old Testament in Greek, published in 1902, Reprint, 2003, Eugene, Oregon, Wipf and Stock Publishers.

Waite, Pastor D. A., Th.D., Ph.D., Defending the King James Bible, 1st Edition, 1992, Collingswood, N.J., Bible For Today Press.

Waite, Pastor D. A., Th.D., Ph.D., Fundamentalist Mis-Information on Bible Versions, Collingswood, N.J., Bible For Today Press.

Waite, Pastor D. A., Th.D., Ph.D., Fuzzy Facts From Fundamentalists on Bible Versions, Collingswood, N.J., Bible For Today Press.

Waite, Pastor D. A., Th.D., Ph.D., Fundamentalist Distortions, Collingswood, N.J., Bible For Today Press.

Webster 1828 Dictionary

Williams, H.D., M.D., Ph.D., The Lie That Changed the Modern World, 2004, Cleveland, GA, The Old Paths Publications, Inc.

ABOUT THE AUTHOR

Dr. Williams was born in Ft. Pierce, Florida, July 11, 1941. He was saved at the age of fourteen at his local Baptist church under Pastor J. R. White where he was active in the church youth group. His local church ordained him to preach the gospel. After graduating with honors from high school, he attended Stetson University where he met his wife, Patricia, and they were married in 1961. Starting in the ministerial program at Stetson and switching to pre-med in his junior year, he graduated with honors with a B.A. After Stetson, he taught high school at Eau Gallie, Florida for two years, and then continued his training at the University of Miami Medical School where he graduated with honors and induction into the AOA medical honorary in his junior year. Following his medical training, Dr. Williams and Patricia settled in New Port Richey, Florida where he practiced Family Medicine as a board-certified family practitioner and was a board-certified emergency room physician. He was active in his community as a hospital board member for twenty years, a chief-of-staff, president of the medical society, an advisory board member and president of Moody Bible Institute's Florida program, a board member of the Health Planning Commission, and a teacher at his local Baptist church. He helped develop and administrate a multi-specialist medical clinic with forty thousand patients and seventeen doctors. He served as Company Commander of a medical unit in the Florida National Guard for nine years. His Biblical training was obtained at Stetson University, Moody Bible Institute, and Louisiana Baptist University. After retirement, Dr. Williams has continued serving the Lord Jesus Christ as an associate pastor, a teacher, a previous vice-president and representative for the Dean Burgon Society, and a member of the King James Bible Research Council. He received a Ph.D. from Louisiana Baptist University. He has traveled to many foreign lands where he has represented the Dean Burgon Society, has taught courses to pastors and has participated in evangelistic events. He is author of the several books, *The Lie That Changed The Modern World; The Miracle of Biblical Inspiration; Word-For-Word Translating of the Received Texts, Verbal Plenary Translating; Hearing the Voice of God; The Septuagint is a Paraphrase; The Pure Words of God; The Attack on the Canon of Scripture; Origin of the Critical Text; Wycliffe Controversies;* and *The Covenant of Salt, The King James Bible's Accuracy & Faithfulness* in addition to many articles and booklets. Some of his articles can be reviewed at this web address: http://www.theoldpathspublications.com/TOPArticles.html.

Dr. Williams and his wife, Patricia have two sons, five grandchildren, and nine great-grandchildren. They recently celebrated their 57th wedding anniversary. He and his wife are the Directors of The Old Paths Publications, which specializes in print-on-demand (POD) books. The purpose of their endeavor is to help authors of Biblically sound books make their works available to the public by reducing the upfront costs of printing, storing, and shipping books by printing the books in the US, England (EU), Australia, and by affiliate printers in many nations, and by making the books available by many distributors such as Amazon worldwide, Barnes and Noble, and others.